A Taste of Silence

A Taste of Silence

Centering Prayer
and the
Contemplative Journey

Carl J. Arico

CONTINUUM • NEW YORK

Dedicated to
Food for the Poor

and in
loving memory of
Mary Mrozowski

2002

The Continuum Publishing Company
370 Lexington Avenue
New York, NY 10017

Printed in the United States of America

Library of Congress Cataloging-in-Publication Data

Arico, Carl J.
    A taste of silence : centering prayer and the contemplative journey
/ Carl J. Arico.
        p.   cm.
    ISBN 0-8264-1106-1
    1. Contemplation.   I. Title
    BV5091.C7A74   1998
    248.3—dc21   98-41406
                                                                         CIP

CONTENTS

Acknowledgments

- To Gene Gollogly for encouraging me to write this book.

- To Fr. Thomas Keating and Gail Fitzpatrick–Hopler for their encouragement and friendship.

- For the house on Long Beach Island, which offered a quiet space to work in.

- To St. Norbert's College for inviting me to do the 1989 lecture series from which the basic material is taken.

- To the over one hundred parishes that have invited me to present my talk on the parish mission, also entitled "A Taste of Silence."

- To Claire and Fred Fox for their gift of final editing.

- To all my friends in Contemplative Outreach who walk with me along the contemplative journey.

Foreword ❖

When most of us look back at our lives, we can identify a person or experience that changed us and made us reevaluate our perspective on life in some profound way. To capture tha dramatic and life-changing nature of these influences we call them turning points, revelations, or conversion experiences. For me, one of these catalyst moments occured some twenty years ago when I "discovered" Centering Prayer. My life has not been the same since.

I make this point because I want readers to understand the tremendous power of the prayer they are about to explore. Yes, there is tremendous value in understanding the history, theology, and personalities associated with Centering Prayer, but the true value of this or any book on the subject is that it ultimately encourages you to embrace the prayer as your own.

I am exicited by Father Carl Arico's book because I believe that it will lead many of you to a life of prayer and deeper relationship with the Lord. In chapters that take the reader through a rich journey of discovery, his guide gives a full perspective on Centering Prayer, its "characters," and its practical application. Few books I have read cover the subject as well or completely.

For me, the highlight of the guide is its chapter on the "true" and "false" self, a theological truth that will be particularly interesting to readers who already practice "centering" but have never heard about this fruit of the prayer. As someone who has prayed daily for many years, I still find the concept of the true and false self as intriguing as ever. The more I study the concept, the more depth I discover there is to explore. For example, before I began my own personal experience with Centering Prayer I never fully appreciated Matthew 10:39: "If you cling to your life, you will lose it; but if you give up your life for me, you will save it."

This is not the only passage of scripture that has become more meaningful to me in light of Centering Prayer's transformative objectives. Another statement by Jesus that is given a renewed meaning is John 14:23: "If a man loves me, he will keep my word, and my Father will love him, and we will come to him and make our home with him." Here, in Christ's own words, the whole purpose for silent prayer is revealed. Through it, we can dwell in the presence of God who is within us.

I share these points only to emphasize again the relevent nature of both Centering Prayer and Father Carl Arico's wonderful guide. As this book makes clear, Centering Prayer is not an archaic part of church's history to be dug up, examined, and set on a shelf as an interesting antiquity. Rather, it's a life-changing tool for our modern lives.

Founder of Food for the Poor
Ferdinard G. Mahfood

Introduction 🕸

It's not that virtue is unimportant, it's just that it is overrated. Don't get me wrong. I'm entirely in favor of virtue and have always admired it, especially at a safe distance. But I have discovered that there is a spirituality beyond virtue as it has come to be known.

I recall my seminary days in the '50s, when a venerated spiritual classic entitled *The Spiritual Life* by Adolphe Tanqueray was our text. The author clearly distinguished three phases of the spiritual life: the purgative, the illuminative, and the unitive. In the purgative phase one worked on overcoming one's sins and even minor faults to develop a life of virtue. The prayer of choice was discursive meditation—reflecting and pondering on the word of God or some spiritual reading. The illuminative phase dealt with the will of God and one's becoming more conscious of the power of grace. The prayer was affective prayer—praying from the heart. The third phase, reserved for a select few, probably mystics, was the unitive way. This phase was the experience of being united with God and one's fellow human beings in abiding love. The prayer was contemplative prayer—a resting in the presence of God.

This was our spirituality text for the four years of theology. After three years of the purgative phase, we were really ready for the higher states. Now in our deacon year—meaning at the end of the year we would be ordained priests—we eagerly awaited the promised glories of the second and third phases. We spent the first half of the school year looking at the illuminative way. It was an enormous relief, raising our eyes from our moral navels, as it were. But to our dismay, Monsignor Baker, our elderly and revered spiritual director, announced that we would not study the unitive phase but go back and review the purgative way, just to make sure we got it right!

His reasoning was pragmatic, not theological. He told us we were going out into a sinful world (1960), a world into which one entered at the peril of coming back less a man. This bit of wisdom was from the Thomas à Kempis classic, *The Imitation of Christ,* but it was a dubious strategy for young men about to engage in the challenge of parish life. Baker announced, "We will leave the unitive way to the contemplative orders. They are the ones really called to that way, not we diocesan priests: we were not called to that. We better go back and review the purgative way."

Baker's real name should have been legion, because that attitude has prevailed in the Catholic Church—in fact in the vast majority of Christian denominations, especially these past few centuries.

I'm writing this book to join many others in telling the rest of the story. The unitive or contemplative way is not reserved for a select few but is a normal development in the life of sincere followers of Christ. I'm writing as a concerned diocesan priest who has been deeply touched in my thirty-eight years of priesthood by the earnest desire of so many to know the contemplative dimension of our tradition. I am tempted to use the word "heritage" rather than "tradition" because heritage is applicable to all Christian denominations. I say this because the heritage flows out of the first one thousand years of Christianity. I will keep to the word, "tradition," but please see it as inclusive and open to all.

I am also writing this book in a spirit of thanksgiving for having had the opportunity to be introduced to the contemplative dimension over twenty years ago through the practice of Centering Prayer. I am grateful too for being exposed to its conceptional background as formulated in a unique way by Fr. Thomas Keating, a Trappist at the monastery of St. Benedict in Snowmass, Colorado.

I see this book as a bridge to many other works that have already been written. An introduction to the introductions. A gathering together of materials and insights into one book concerning the practice of Centering Prayer and its conceptual background, as well as the historical setting from which the prayer comes. I was told that what was needed was a down-to-earth presentation by a person with pastoral experience. Well, that is quite a challenge, but with God's help and the help of many of my friends, I hope that request has been fulfilled in the following pages.

How did I get involved in the Centering Prayer movement? Let me tell the story. It was my custom since 1969 to make my annual retreat at St. Joseph's Trappist Monastery in Spencer, Massachusetts. The routine was as follows: a monk gave us a short talk in the morning; we spent the rest of the day joining the community in the praying of the office and entering into monastic silence. In 1975 our retreat master was Fr. William Meninger. I knew him because he was a former diocesan priest who became a Trappist. I enjoyed needling him for escaping into the monastery and not having the courage to stay out in the real world with real people. Those of you who know Fr. William know that he holds his own with no trouble during our friendly exchanges. On this retreat he introduced us to Centering Prayer. On our three-and-a-half-hour drive back to New Jersey, I and two other priest friends discussed how moved we were by the experience and the conceptual background of Centering Prayer. We decided to meet once a month to support one another in the prayer. It was a real turning point for me and for them. The group has grown to ten priests who still meet monthly. I must confess that since working full time with Contemplative Outreach since 1987, I don't get to all the meetings because I am sometimes out of town. But I am there in spirit, and my brother priests know it and support me with their prayers.

But I am getting ahead of myself; let's continue the story.

Right from the beginning I kept in contact with Thomas Keating who was then abbot at St. Joseph's and supported his monks there in this work. I was placed on the mailing list and attended their training programs for presenters that were sponsored by the monastery. William Meninger put together a series of tapes on Centering Prayer, which I used with small groups in the parish with good results. In the late '70s I began giving retreats to priests and set aside time during the retreat to present Centering Prayer. I was amazed at the good response I got from my brother priests. I was at that time active in the Family Life Ministry for the Archdiocese of Newark. I found that when I shared Centering Prayer with couples and with the separated and divorced on my retreats, many were genuinely taken by it. My interest and involvement continued to grow, and in 1983 I was invited by Fr. Keating to attend a special fifteen-day retreat with a group of Christians to intensively practice Centering Prayer. That was a major breakthrough on so many levels for the group of twelve and for me. I became aware of how powerful Centering Prayer was because it was a container for my consenting to not only God's presence in my life, but also God's action in my life. We affectionately call the retreat Lama I after the name of the retreat center in New Mexico. Even though I had been faithful to the prayer since 1975, my commitment intensified. It seemed that God was working on me at a much deeper level. I continued to spread the good news. In 1984 I became a founding member of Contemplative Outreach and, along with Fr. Keating, a member of the board of trustees of Contemplative Outreach Ltd., the service arm of the Contemplative Outreach network.

Since 1987 I've been working with Contemplative Outreach full time with the blessing of Archbishop Theodore McCarrick of Newark, my diocese.

Let me share the vision statement of Contemplative Outreach with you because it will place the book in a larger context.

> Contemplative Outreach is a spiritual network of individuals and small faith communities committed to living the contemplative dimension of the Gospel in everyday life through the practice of Centering Prayer. The contemplative dimension of the Gospel manifests itself in an ever-deepening union with the living Christ and the practical caring for others that flows from that relationship.

Our purpose is to share the method of Centering Prayer and its immediate conceptual background. We also encourage the practice of *lectio divina,* particularly its movement into Contemplative Prayer, which a regular and established practice of Centering Prayer facilitates.

We identify with the Christian Contemplative Heritage. While we are formed by our respective denominations, we are united in our common search for God and the experience of the living Christ through Centering Prayer. We affirm our solidarity with the contemplative dimension of other religions and sacred traditions, with the needs and rights of the whole human family, and with all creation.

Let me highlight some of the main points of the vision statement. We are a spiritual network; we do not see ourselves as an organization. The common bond between the members is a desire to live the contemplative dimension of the gospel through the practice of Centering Prayer and *lectio divina* in its movement toward contemplative prayer. There is no doubt in our minds that what we are about is grounded in our Christian contemplative heritage. We use the word "heritage" because it is broader than our individual traditions—we are feeding off the same common source. We are ecumenical and at the same time feel a sense of solidarity with other religions and traditions when they manifest their contemplative interests. Because of this contemplative grounding there is a sense of oneness with all God's people and all God's creation.

In light of my last statement I have dedicated the book to Food for the Poor. Its founder Ferdie Mahfood is an example of the power of Centering Prayer that moved him to hear the cry of the poor, leave his professional job with his family's exporting firm, and direct his attention and expertise to the poor, especially in Haiti and the Caribbean.

I have also placed the book in memory of Mary Mrozowski, the first lady of Centering Prayer, who died suddenly in 1993 while giving a series of "Letting Go Workshops." I have never met a person so open to the Spirit as Mary. She taught me and many others that the only thing that really matters is one's love of God. In her New Yorker way I can hear her say, "If you got that, you got it all, so what's the problem?"

I would like to recommend three books as background reading to this book: *Open Mind, Open Heart* by Fr. Thomas Keating, *Too Deep for Words* by Sr. Thelma Hall, and *The Cloud of Unknowing* prepared by William Johnson. I will refer to other books as needed.

Finally, I want to mention that one of my favorite radio personalities is the commentator Paul Harvey. He has a comment which he makes that has caught the imagination of many—after presenting the facts of a news story, he will pause and then say, "In a moment the rest of the story." What he then presents puts a whole new light on the story; in fact, many times he turns it around and makes it understandable on a deeper level. This is what my friends like to call me—Fr. Paul Harvey—sharing the "rest of the story." So let's look at the rest of the story with regard to our contemplative Christian tradition.

May I offer a suggestion? Before each chapter and especially before each time you read, you might consider sitting in Centering Prayer for ten minutes or so. Reading about prayer is beneficial, but the experience of prayer deepens your understanding. Read the chapter on the method of Centering Prayer or refer to the appendix for the leaflet on Centering Prayer so that you can enter into the experience of the prayer.

1 ❀

Making a Spiritual Quilt: Clarification of Terms

"Making a spiritual quilt" is a good image. What are the elements, the pieces that make up this contemplative dimension of the gospel? I have been fascinated watching the making of a quilt, how the pieces fit together and how some pieces that look like scrap or just the trimmings (nothing is wasted) become the finishing touches that give the quilt a look of elegance.

So let's look at some of the pieces. We are members of the *human family*. We experience and live with the human condition. We have a past, present, and a future and we cannot lose sight of this. We are culturally conditioned by the who, the what, the when, the why, and the where of our lives. It is in this ground that our God works through and with us and in spite of us.

We are part of something bigger than ourselves which takes many names: family, country, race, gender, religion, church, and so on. The older we get, the more we realize we need more than ourselves. We are not on the journey by ourselves and yet it is easy to act as though we are. We realize that we need redemption and transformation. So God has offered us a *religious community, a church,* with sacraments and liturgy or at least ritual of some kind. The invitation is there, for there is a deep yearning in each person to belong, a place to gather to express that belief and to

give honor and worship to God. Some sort of structure or insti-
tution is needed in all our lives. We fight it, we move away from
it, we try to live without it, and yet in the important moments of
our lives we are drawn back to it.

Another part of our spiritual quilt is a need for a *belief system*—a dogma, a theology, a creed—some would call it a conceptual background for life, a getting in touch with the wisdom
of our faith and an integrating of it with our present knowledge. A creative tension always exists between the two—the
wisdom of the past and the knowledge of the present. This is
healthy. I find I am always amazed at the insight and wisdom of
those who have gone before me in the Christian tradition. They
had more of a grasp on life than the little for which I had given
them credit. There is always something new that we need to
learn from them. There is a need for all of us to return to the
roots of our own faith. For example, I have been impressed by
many of the Eastern teachers who urge their followers to find
themselves a wisdom teacher in their own tradition. I recall a
story of a Catholic woman who for a number of years was
studying under a Zen master. One day he said to her, "Go find
yourself a Trappist monk. You must be true to your roots." She
was shocked to hear this, but shortly after this comment was
made, she started reading Thomas Merton and was reunited
with her Catholic faith—reunited on a different level as a result
of her experience in Zen meditation. Some relate this "crossing
over" to an experiencing of another religion or tradition as a
stage in the return to one's original roots and seeing it in a
much different way. St. Paul hinted at that when he said "When
I was a child, I spoke as a child . . ." but that as an adult, he
saw things differently.

The third patch of our spiritual quilt is our need for the *mystical dimension of spirituality*. Mystical is a word that conjures up
all sort of images. I see living mystically as deepening the beliefs
and practices of our faith by allowing the Spirit to recreate us. I
call this the incarnational journey. I am not talking about leaving
the practice and beliefs of our faith, but about movement into a
space where our wills and emotions are engaged. Our practices

and beliefs become enfleshed in the reality of the experiences of everyday life.

Practices and beliefs are important, but we cannot get stuck there. We grasp the direction that we need to go and we head out on the journey. If we get too caught up with only the practices and beliefs only, in my view, we never really get started on the journey. For those of us who do this, spiritual practices become the goal and focus of the spiritual journey. We act like a person who wants to go on a hiking trip. We keep checking our compass, but we don't trust the compass; it may not be accurate, so we get a new one, and then another one because we want to be sure this is the right direction. What happens is we never venture out on the journey. Practices and beliefs are essential, but the journey goes beyond us. I have heard it put this way: we move from a religious conversion to a personal conversion, which brings us greater intimacy with God.

A fourth patch is *our need to be of service to others*. When we see the world as it is, we see that we have a need to make a contribution of ourselves to help better the world. There is a saying that all genuine prayer leads to genuine action, and all genuine action leads back to genuine prayer. Love of neighbor, as one loves oneself is known to everyone to be one of the great commandments. There is another Scripture which says that we should love our neighbor as Christ loves us. This is where the whole issue of doing for others out of a spirit of compassion and utmost charity comes into play. Thomas Merton often emphasizes the point that too much good is being done, not in the name of the other, but in the name of one's self.

> He who attempts to act and do things for others or for the world without deepening his own self-understanding, freedom, integrity and capacity to love, will not have anything to give others. He will communicate to them nothing but the contagion of his own obsessions, his aggressiveness, his ego-centered ambition, his delusions about ends and means, his doctrinaire prejudices and ideas. There is nothing more tragic in the modern world than the misuse of power and action to which men are driven by their own misunderstandings and misapprehensions . . . we are more alienated and estranged from the inner ground of meaning and of love than we

have ever been. The result is evident . . . this crisis is centered pre-
cisely in the country that has made a fetish out of action and has
lost (or perhaps never had) the sense of contemplation.(Thomas
Merton, *Contemplation in a World of Action,* Image, 1973, 178–79)

The end result, too many times, is that the present state is
worse than the past. Service to others demands a serious inven-
tory of our own motivations and reliance on prayer.

And so we see in our personal spiritual quilt the need to
belong, the need to have something to believe in, an openness to
the mystical elements in our lives, and the need to be of service
to others. *In religious terms these elements are church, creed, sacraments, and service.* The church provides the gathering space for
believers to come together in worship and prayer. The creed gives
us a conceptual background to rely on other than our own ideas
and beliefs. The sacraments remind us of the mystical aspects of
the important events of our lives. Service to others celebrates that
we are one family and that although many, we are really one. It
has been said that a fully developed, properly balanced spiritual
life must be the result of a harmonious blending of these four elements, no one of which may be neglected, except at the cost of a
one-sided, distorted, enfeebled spiritual life.

I would like to add here some new pieces to our spiritual
quilt with some observations about the spiritual journey, spirituality, spiritual exercises, and prayer itself.

The *spiritual journey* is life, the events of everyday life. God
speaks to us and works on us through the events of everyday life.
We would like to make our lives neat but they don't work out
that way. Life is messy when we really live it. Oh, we would like
it to be clean, ordered, and sterilized. Nature tells us that nothing
grows in a sterile environment. Every gardener knows that dirt
and worms are crucial for a healthy garden. Every mother knows
we were born in blood, sweat, and tears. All new births are a bit
messy and very painful. Let me tell you a story. A good number
of years ago part of my annual vacation was spent camping. A few
friends and I traveled throughout the United States each summer
enjoying the experience of camping. One year we were at Crater
Lake, Oregon. I went out to do some fishing at the lake. A park

ranger came by and told me, "You will never catch anything in this lake." I thought he was joking. I said to him that would not be unusual, since I never seem to catch anything anywhere. He looked at me and said, "I am serious: you will not catch anything in this lake; the water is too pure to sustain life." Goodness. "Too pure to sustain life": sterile, great to look at, but not life-giving. What an insight for the spiritual life. The "stuff" of our life is the "stuff" that our God uses to feed us, catch us, and reel us in. This has certainly given me a whole new way of looking at the spiritual life. I will talk more about that later.

For many years I have searched for a good description of *spirituality* that speaks to the contemporary person. Better still, that speaks to me. When I was on sabbatical in Rome in 1986, I attended a course on spiritual direction taught by a Jesuit named Herbie Alfonso at the Gregorian University. It was an excellent course. Here is his description of spirituality as I recall it: "It is individual women or men who are animated by the living presence of the Trinity on how they act and react habitually and spontaneously to the everyday events of their lives according to their vocation in life and their gifts." Notice the depth of the description. A human being is one who acknowledges the indwelling of the Trinity consenting to not only the presence but also the action of God because we are temples of the Holy Spirit. This consent is lived out in the everyday events of our lives and how we act and react habitually and spontaneously to those events. It means that there is a pattern of behavior in us that shows itself in the give-and-take of life. This pattern of behavior is either gospel- or worldly-based. Our responses to life show our value systems. There is then a challenge to live out of our vocation—single, married, religious, or priesthood—and to use the many gifts which God has given to us. Alfonso's description of spirituality makes it a fluid, on-going, and dynamic model to follow. I ask you to consider this observation: show me what is going on in your life and how you are responding to it and you are showing me what the Lord wants you to bring to prayer for healing, forgiveness, and celebration. I have come to use these terms—healing, forgiveness, and celebration—for a definite purpose. When we look at

life, we need to see its potential no matter what the circumstances. There are opportunities for the healing of deep hurts or
memories. There are opportunities for forgiveness—how long
can we hold on to some situations in our lives? We can rational-
ize, justify, and glorify the reasons for not forgiving, but in the
end who gets hurt? We do—the non-forgivers. While we are
looking at these healings and forgivings, all too often, we forget
the celebration of life and all that is going right. In any genuine
spiritual journey, healing, forgiveness, and celebration are all part
of the spiritual landscape.

I would like to talk now about our *spiritual exercises*. What
do I mean by spiritual exercises? I mean our collection of prayers,
devotions, and spiritual practices that make up the posturing of
ourselves before God. These exercises are "keys" to open us to
greater intimacy with God. Although they are important, they are
not as important as the relationship to which they open us. We
need to look beyond the prayers we say or devotions we attend,
just as we look beyond the bread we eat and the wine we drink
at the Eucharist. If we stay within these formal exercises, there is
a danger we will become mere maintenance persons. I think of
school maintenance workers walking the halls. They carry with
them a large ring of keys. These keys can open all the doors of the
building. Theirs is quite a powerful position; this is only appreciated when they lose their keys. The ring of keys is so large that
they walk lop-sided—tilting to one side. They open all the classroom doors but never go in to take the courses that are offered.
They put the key in the door, unlock it, open the door, and walk
away. They have done their job. They do not bring themselves;
they only bring their keys. They are satisfied with only a surface
encounter: as I said, they never take the courses. You can say that
it is not their job, and that is true. The point that I am making is
that although they are in the school, they are not taking full
advantage of what the school is offering.

Let's apply this to our spiritual exercises. You have heard
people say, "I got my prayers in today." What are they saying?
They are saying just that: they got them in and perhaps just
barely. Let's picture ourselves as maintenance workers of prayer

with our ring of many prayers and devotions. We put the key in and say our prayers. We turn the key to open ourselves to a deeper relationship with God. In other words, we do not take the course the Lord wants to teach us. There is a wonderful story told about a student who was studying the Torah. One day he came to his teacher and told him "I have gone through the Torah, so what is next?" The teacher said to him, "Next it is for the Torah to go through you." So one can say, "I got my prayers in; I went through my prayers." The answer back could be, "Did the prayers go through you?" You may ask then how do I let my prayers go through me? I will discuss in the chapter on *lectio divina* how the ancient tradition of praying the Scriptures, when properly understood, can be applied to our spiritual exercises.

A person can say a lot of prayers faithfully each day, but if they only "get their prayers in," very little is going to happen in their lives. They are maintaining a "prayer life" but they are not "alive in their prayer life." They are not entering the classroom of prayer.

I believe that our prayers, when prayed and not just "gotten in," give us the "eyes and ears" to see God working in the events of our everyday lives. Remember what Jesus said, "Those who have eyes to see will see, those who have ears to hear will hear." Our prayers are a cry for improved seeing and hearing. Don't be surprised by what you will see and hear.

Now let's talk about *prayer itself*. I find Father Armand Nigro's description of prayer exciting.

> Prayer is principally *God's work, God's gift*. He is present as our Father, loving life into us, sustaining and working in us. He is in every heartbeat, every breath, every expanse of physical, sexual and psychic energy, every thought, hope and desire, every decision. When we are conscious of God's presence, of God being in and around us, we are in prayer. When we are aware that we move and love in God's loving gaze, we are in prayer. When God makes us conscious of God's nearness and touch, we are in prayer. In prayer, we are not called to support or enrich God but to be fed and strengthened by God.

Notice how the focus is not on our efforts but on the activity of God. Prayer is God's work and God's gift. God is initiating the encounter. It is being done for our good, not the good of God. We are not doing a favor for God, we are in praying doing a favor for ourselves. This kind of receptivity is extremely difficult for most people in our culture. It is hard to admit that it is God who takes the initiative and it is our role to respond. It is not only while we are praying but it goes on throughout the day, in all of our activities.

In prayer, we are called to let go of control of our lives into God's hands—to relax and be with God, letting God be with us and communicate with us in any way God prefers. God is the loving Lord of the Universe, the Lord of History, the Lord of our lives. In Him all things live and move and have their being. Awareness of God's presence enables us to see all things as relating to God. We see the world with fresh eyes and ears.

I have a confession to make to you. I have a desire to have you take a second look—better yet, a serious look—at your habits of prayer. No matter what you are doing, there is always room for improvement. I ask you this question, "Is prayer making you more conscious, more aware of the presence of the divine in your life?" Of course, I can't put a face on the divine in reality, but I can arrive at a different experience of seeing and hearing. Is it not possible that instead of finding God in all things we divide the world into compartments? We say, "Now I'm going to do something holy—say my prayers." Then, afterwards, " Now I turn my attention to survival needs: paying bills, administrivia, and all sorts of other things. I hurry through them so I can go back and be with God and do God's work." This is a bad split of God's world. Do you remember the catechism question, "Where is God?"—where we answered with great gusto, "God is everywhere." So why don't we really believe that? All of reality is saturated with the presence and power of God. Everything we do is a potential playing field for prayer.

Our spiritual quilt now has some additional patches. I have added the *spiritual life,* which is God working in the events of everyday life; *spirituality,* which is our habitual way of acting and reacting to these events of life that show us where our values are; and our *spiritual exercises,* which have many purposes but are done each day to give us the eyes to see and the ears to hear how the Lord is working in our lives. Then *prayer* itself, which is God's work and God's gift to us.

I now want to share the two approaches to prayer in our Christian tradition because they help set the stage to explore the reason why this book is called *A Taste of Silence*. One approach to prayer is the kataphatic and the other is the apophatic. Goodness! How about those words? Well, they are not as awesome as they sound.

The first approach, the *kataphatic,* is the one we know best. It is prayer that is made up of words, concepts, images, and resolutions. We pray, we pay attention to what we pray, we examine our conscience, we resolve to do better, we acknowledge our faults, and then we go out and try to live what we prayed.

The word "kataphatic" is from the two Greek words *Kata* meaning "down," and *phasis* which means "speech." So the kataphatic tradition speaks of divinity in the only way we know how, by "talking down," in the sense of using our knowledge, words, images, and senses.

The kataphatic tradition is the way of affirmation with the emphasis on similarities between God and creatures. In this tradition we discuss prayer as a relationship. We study what goes into a human relationship and then apply those principles and insights to our prayer relationship. In this approach, we affirm what we see and know. Only then do we realize that God is more and beyond all that we see and know. This tradition affirms concepts, images, and symbols. The classic saintly witness to this tradition is St. Ignatius of Loyola. In our day, Teilhard de Chardin stands out as a leading proponent. We go through creation to God and God is present in creation.

Then there is another balancing attitude and approach to prayer, the *apophatic* tradition. The Greek word *"apophani"* means to mention something by saying what an object is "not." The apophatic tradition tends to be speechless, to be wordless. It senses that speech is as helpless to describe God as the eyes are at looking into the sun. This is the approach of surrender to the infinite, of losing one's center to find it. This is the approach of paradox, verbal modesty, and finally silence. This is the approach of surrender, of receptivity on the deepest level.

The apophatic tradition is the way of negation which emphasizes the radical differences that exist between God and us. God is best reached by forgetting, by unknowing, without support of concepts, images, or symbols.

Our understanding of God in this way emphasizes the difference between us and God. No matter what example I use, my words cannot really capture the who and what of God. My finite faculties can never grasp God with my intellect. I finally admit that I am finite and God is infinite and in the end all I can do is rest in God's presence, be in God's presence, surrender to God— God who is beyond all my speculations. We know what God is not, more than what God is. Our mind becomes dark, without the support of images, concepts, or symbols. The two great witnesses in this tradition are the author of *The Cloud of Unknowing* and St. John of the Cross. Thomas Merton also stands largely in this tradition.

Neither the kataphatic nor the apophatic tradition is absolute. It is a matter of emphasis between the two, not opposition. No matter how negatively we approach our knowledge of God, we always use words that require human thought. And no matter how much we rely on sacrament and symbol and the revealed word in scripture to affirm God's presence, we acknowledge that we really are talking about a God who is beyond us. Together, the two traditions create the total picture of prayer.

The apophatic approach encourages us to release the limiting images, which limit our prayer life. The kataphatic tradition points out we have to have images to drop: we have to have knowledge to go beyond it.

Don't try to decide between them. The two approaches need and depend on each other and we need and depend on both of them. The kataphatic approach can best be represented by the tradition of *lectio divina*. In terms of the apophatic approach I will be focusing on a spiritual classic, *The Cloud of Unknowing,* and particularly a prayer called "Centering Prayer." These will all be discussed later in the book.

The next piece to be added to the spiritual quilt is the term *contemplation*. The classic meaning of contemplation is "resting in God." There are two types of contemplation: acquired and infused. The terms acquired contemplation and infused contemplation are terms from the past that fell out of use but are being looked at again. I have always found them important for the proper understanding of what contemplation is all about. I find it also helpful in describing the practice of Centering Prayer. To put it simply, acquired contemplation is the effort we put in under the prompting of the Spirit to rest in the presence of God. This effort can be quite concentrative or it can be quite receptive. Examples of the *concentrative* are discursive meditation, rosary, stations of the cross, veneration of icons, visual (guided imagery) meditation, and affective prayer, which is a mulitplication of aspirations. In the concentrative there is the use of our faculties (imagination, intellect, will) to produce an effect of resting in the presence of God. Examples of the *receptive* could be the Jesus Prayer, the simple repetition of an aspiration, Christian Zen prayer, or Christian meditation, which is the repetition of a mantra and Centering Prayer.

I know that seems a bit confusing, but a comparison will help. In *concentrative* acquired contemplation, you are concentrating; with *receptive* acquired contemplation, you aren't. In *concentrative* acquired contemplation you are active; with *receptive* acquired contemplation you are primarily receptive. The initiative is always God's. In *concentrative* acquired contemplation if you get an insight, you hang on to it, you remember it, you think, you feel certain emotions, you employ your imagination, you are aware, you are the active agent, you are in control, or so it seems. In *receptive* acquired contemplation, you become remarkably receptive, you don't try to understand, you don't try to feel anything, you surrender, you consent. If you get an insight, you let it go. In a sense, you simply want to be letting everything else go for the sake of resting in the Lord.

People who can relax and enjoy this kind of contemplation have something happen in their lives. As they become more and more comfortable with simple prayer forms, they begin to feel uncomfortable with the wordiness of prayer talk, either privately or in community. It is a process of being weaned away from discursive meditation. (If you are not familiar with the literature on prayer, discursive meditation is structured, beginning with self-examination, developing a spiritual theme, and usually concluding with resolutions that will improve moral behavior.) "Weaned away from" doesn't mean the former was bad or even inadequate; it does mean we are maturing in prayer. We do not stop praying these prayers. They are still an important part of our prayer life. But we are no longer satisfied with the many words of prayer or many words of scripture. There is a simplification taking place— more is *not* better.

Infused contemplation is a gift from the Holy Spirit. What happens is that the spirit sees the effort we are making to rest in God's presence. We can only go so far on our own. Then the spirit takes over and brings us to a deeper rest. All prayer is a gift from God. But prayers differs in degree when looked at in terms of how much effort and concentration we contribute on our part and how much the Spirit controls it on Her part.

Thomas Keating puts it this way [the bracketed statements are mine]:

> The development of one's relationship with Christ to the point of communing beyond words, thoughts, feelings and the multiplication of particular acts; a process moving from the simplified activity of waiting upon God [receptive acquired contemplation] to the ever-increasing predominance of the Gifts of the Spirit as the source of one's prayer [infused contemplation].

It's easier to talk about acquired contemplation: I did this, it had this effect, and I'm going to do that. With infused contemplation, all I really know is that I was there. Not much else other than some level of intimacy. A level of communication happens that we can only talk about in poetry, image, and allegory. Perhaps it's like being on the dance floor late at night, our faculties have been captured by the music, we're relaxed, we've entered into the spirit of the experience. We are moving without effort, without flaw. In the dance of prayer we are united, one with God. From this loving union flows a loving knowledge transcending abstract conceptual knowledge. The infused quality of this loving knowledge indicates that it is wholly a gift from God and is totally beyond human capacity. No strictly human effort can bring it about. All we know is that we are experiencing this oneness. It is pure gift.

Teilhard de Chardin states it this way, "To lose oneself in the unfathomable, to plunge into the inexhaustible, to find peace in the incorruptible, to give of one's deepest to him whose depths have no end."

Then what is the role of *Centering Prayer* [brackets are mine]?

Centering prayer [receptive acquired contemplation] is a method designed to facilitate the development of contemplative prayer by preparing our faculties to cooperate with this gift [infused contemplation]. It is an attempt to present the teaching of earlier time [e.g., *The Cloud of Unknowing* and other apophatic teachings] in an updated form and to put a certain order and regularity into it. It is not meant to replace other kinds of prayer; it simply puts other kinds of prayer into a new and fuller perspective. During the time of prayer we consent to God's presence and action within. At other times [outside the prayer time] our attention moves outward to discover God's presence everywhere. (From leaflet, "The Method of Centering Prayer" by Thomas Keating)

I will be talking more about Centering Prayer later in the book. The important point here is that it is not infused contemplation but receptive acquired contemplation. A prayer preparing one to receive the gift of infused contemplation, if the Spirit chooses to do so.

So we have added to our spiritual quilt the insights of *acquired contemplation,* which can be concentrative and receptive, and *infused contemplation,* which is a gift from the Holy Spirit, and the role of *Centering Prayer.*

Let us end by exploring what is meant by *transformation* so that we can finish this part of our spiritual quilt.

In Scripture we hear about "new creation," "born again," "I live now not I but Christ lives in me," "unless you are born again of water and the Holy Spirit you will not enter the kingdom of God." The new life we are called to has been called "transformation" by contemporary writers. Let's turn our attention to the process of transformation. A few distinctions may be in order. I understand transformation to be a restructuring of consciousness which takes place, empowering one to perceive, relate, and respond with increasing sensitivity to the divine presence through and beyond everything that exists. That is quite a mouthful. Simply put it means a complete overhauling by the Spirit within each of us. The liturgy has a fine summation: "Through Him and with Him and in Him in the unity of the Holy Spirit, all honor and glory is Yours almighty Father, forever and ever. Amen."

The contemplative is aware of God's presence in everything. After a while it becomes difficult to make a judgment on what is "bad" or "good" in one's life. What I mean by that is sometimes what seems "bad" to us, or difficult, turns out to be an important moment of growth in our lives opening us to a greater reality. Sometimes what seems "good" turns out to be an obstacle on the journey. It is hard to discern all the time but one thing is sure, something new requires breaking of the old mold. As the potter breaks the old mold in order to replace it with a new one, so must we let go of the old self and replace it with the new.

We create an awful tension within ourselves when we take in only part of the message of the Scriptures. Many see fidelity to God to be the path to peace and harmony—yes, but it is also the path of unrest when we must change our preconceived notions of what life is all about. It means accepting the uncertainties of the journey. For example, when John of the Cross (sixteenth-century mystic and doctor of the Church) talks about the dark night as God's transforming process. The dark is our resistance and the night is God's purifying power. We experience the dark when we don't want to change. The darkness is our contribution to the process. We arm wrestle with God and fight against changing with all our might.

Transformation, the process of God's recreating of our very selves, is characterized by three phases.

The first phase is *simple transformation,* which takes place because of our desire and our willingness to consent to the changes. We remain in control. No surprises here. We have our prayer routine, we keep to a good and healthy schedule each day. There are habits in our lives that we know need to be eliminated and others that need to be enriched. We feel responsible for what needs to be done within us.

The second phase of the process of transformation is *transitional transformation,* which means that although we have a desire and we are active agents in our own cause, we start to feel out of control. It is a subtle change that begins to take place. Have you ever found yourself getting confused? You weren't as sure of yourself as you were in the past? When the good old answers weren't working any more. Or have you found yourself feeling blasphemous because you were so angry with God? Or worse than anger, just apathetic, just dead inside? Or were you tormented with inclinations quite contrary to your committed monogamous or celibate life? In this transitional stage, you feel out of control, you feel you're losing your dedication, you even feel as if you are falling apart. If you are faithful to your prayer life and your responsibilities, you are not; God is moving you into a new way of life. You need to learn that you are not always in control. God is moving you into a new way of life. It does not feel that way but it is true. Many run from this experience of brokenness. We fear it, naturally, yet it is part of the process of transformation.

The last phase is *radical transformation*. In this phase we are completely out of control, we are no longer in charge. God has taken over and is working on levels of our being that we cannot get to. The Divine Physician is performing deep spiritual surgery on us. The surgery is getting to the root of the "stuff" inside us that prevents us from seeing and hearing the gospel.

All these phases of transformation are not done through our strategies. They're being done to us because we are open to remaining in the presence of God. We become open to become what we are called to be.

Our transformation begins to become progressively more apparent to people around us without our knowing it. We don't feel it. They do. In a certain sense, in our transformation we become Christ for those who can sense the transformation. Many times we come away from a retreat and say something like "As a result of this retreat, I'm going to be more loving." Then someone will come up to us a few months later and say, "Gee, you're much more loving." Our answer might be, "Yes, I'm working on that." With this radical transformation, I'm talking about something we are not aware of, something we are not "working on." So if someone were to come up to you and say, "You seem to be more lovable," you're answer is apt to be, "Really, I am? Thank you for telling me." We were not even aware of it. The Spirit was working on us and we did not even know it. But we know it now, it had to be brought to our attention.

So this completes our spiritual quilt: some things to keep in mind as you read this book. Come back to check this chapter out if you need to as you read. Remember that into our quilt we have incorporated the need to belong (Church), the need to have something to believe in (Creed), the need to be open to the mystical (Sacraments), the need to be of service to others, spiritual life, spirituality, spiritual exercises, prayer itself, the kataphatic and apophatic approaches to prayer, acquired (concentrative and receptive) and infused contemplation, the role of Centering Prayer, and the levels of transformation—simple, transitional, and radical. Yes, I know: a lot of words. You are right, but it is fun to talk about what we love the most.

As I said, I have been fascinated with the making of a quilt, how the pieces fit together, and how pieces that look like scrap become the finishing touches. Add your own pieces, perhaps even your own trimmings, as you read. Each of you can bring your own experiences and needs. Be creative. Don't say, "He should have said this or that." Add it, make it complete for you.

2 ❈

Superstars of the Christian Tradition

In *Open Mind Open Heart,* Fr. Thomas Keating said:

> Centering Prayer is an effort to renew the teaching of the Christian tradition on contemplative prayer. It is an attempt to present that tradition in an up-to-date form and to put a certain order and method into it. Like the word contemplation, the term centering prayer has come to have a variety of meanings. For the sake of clarity it seems best to reserve the term centering prayer for the specific method of preparing for the gift of contemplation.

As part of dealing with the fundamentals of Centering Prayer it is important to look at the tradition. The discovery of the Christian contemplative tradition has been an exciting adventure for me. I love history and I have been fascinated by the insights and wisdom of the spiritual writers of our tradition. I like to refer to them as our superstars. I have selected a few that I feel are important in developing the apophatic approach to prayer (receptive acquired contemplation) which leads to the gift of infused contemplation. I believe that Centering Prayer comes out of this apophatic tradition.

I invite you to read these spiritual writers, reflect on their wisdom and pray with them.

Some friends of mine, while talking about my plans for this book, said to me, "Why do you want to include this material? A

lot of people could care less about what someone said in the
fourth century—why don't you drop it? Move on to the practical
matters." Well, you can imagine how taken back I was when they
spoke this way about my "good friends" in our Christian tradition. But knowing that there could be some truth to their observation, let me say this: If this is not your cup of tea, or if you
would like to come back to my "good friends" later, then you
have my permission to skip this chapter and move on.

Imagine ourselves at a Sunday brunch in a fine restaurant.
We are pleased to be here: it is a relaxing day and we are taking our time picking and choosing as little or as much as we
would like, knowing that we can not taste everything. So let's
enjoy the brunch.

Each of these spiritual masters has his or her own angle, vision
and approach to the apophatic tradition. All have been influenced
by passages in the scripture that call for a resting and waiting in the
Lord. Here is a sampling of quotes from the Psalms.

Ps 46:10	Be still and know that I am God
Ps 37:7	Be still before the Lord and wait patiently for Him
Ps 62:1	My soul finds rest in God alone.
Ps 131:2	But I stilled and quieted my soul; like a weaned child with its mother, like a weaned child is my soul within me.
Ps 27:14	Wait for the Lord, be strong and let your heart take courage, yes, wait for the Lord.
Ps 33:20	Our soul waits for the Lord; He is our help and shield.
Ps 62:1,5	For God alone my soul waits in silence; from Him comes my salvation. . . . For God alone my soul waits in silence; for my help is from Him.

Now to some of the spiritual masters:

The first is St. Gregory of Nyssa, (330–95) a fourth-century
monk. In his approach, he has taken the life of Moses and made
it a paradigm of the spiritual journey. Gregory noted that Moses
went up the mountain into the light to meet the Lord and then
descended back to the valley where he had to deal with darkness

and confusion. It may be worthwhile to read this encounter with God in the Old Testament. It can give great comfort.

Moses' experience was profound and the cost was great. In the end he never entered the promised land. He could only see it in the distance. We never completely experience the promised land, either. We keep moving toward it, but we never enter: entrance comes only with death. Yet we are already there: God is within us and we don't fully appreciate the divine presence in us right now.

Gregory has a marvelous passage in which Moses says, "God, I have done everything you've asked me to do. I have only one request to make of you. I want to see your face. That's all I ask."

As Moses asks to see the face of God, God moves toward Moses, but as he gets close, He covers Moses' face with His hand. Moses cannot see God's face, but as God retreats he catches a glimpse of God's back. So Moses has to follow God from behind. "Come, follow me."

God will not let Moses dictate the terms of the relationship or manipulate Him. He wants Moses to follow Him. God requires that Moses trust God's terms of the relationship. This is a good example for our prayer lives. We don't make the rules; we follow them. We don't dictate the terms; we surrender to them. We don't see God's face; we follow along behind. That's the nature of the prayer relationship.

St. Gregory recounts that he came to know that none of those things apprehended by sense perception and contemplated by the understanding really subsist. Only the transcendent essence and cause of the universe on which everything depends subsists:

> The Divine Nature, whatever it may be in itself surpasses every mental concept. For it is altogether inaccessible to reasoning and conjecture, nor has there been found any human faculty capable of perceiving the incomprehensible for we cannot devise a means for understanding inconceivable things. Therefore the great apostles calls His way "unsearchable" (Rom 11:33) meaning that the way that leads to the knowledge of the Divine Essence is inaccessible to thought. (*The Beatitudes*, Sermon 6, 146–47)

Put simply, all that we can perceive and know never can capture the "essence of God." Our perception of God is like a finger pointing to the real thing or at least pointing in the right direction.

That reminds me of a story—I believe it was told by Anthony de Mello, a contemporary Jesuit spiritual writer—about a holy person who was leaving the people to whom he had ministered for years, to go to another place. In his final talk he told them, pointing his finger at the cross, "Don't forget the importance of the cross in your life." Many years later he was passing by and decided to visit them. When he was getting close to their place of worship, he could hear their singing and praise of God. He felt so pleased that the community was still alive and worshipping with such great joy and enthusiasm. As he entered the church, however, his face dropped and he was filled with sadness. They were worshipping the finger and not the cross; they were worshipping the means and not the end. There is a danger of getting so attached to our prayers that we forget our relationship with God.

Gregory also makes this same important point:

> For the present congregation needs instruction not so much on how to pray, as on the necessity of praying at all, a necessity that has perhaps not been grasped by most people. (*The Lord's Prayer*, Sermon 1, par. 21)

Does this ring a bell? Remember, he is speaking to a fourth-century congregation, so he makes some important points. First, that we come to God in prayer on God's terms not our own. Second, that our concepts and ideas cannot ever grasp the essence of God, which means they lead us to silence in God's presence; in a sense, we are speechless. Third, as important as learning how to pray is; it is more important to have the desire to pray—or, as he says, the necessity to pray.

Now to Evagrius Ponticus (346–99), an interesting man who was one of the most articulate of the desert fathers. The desert fathers and mothers were men and women who, after the Emperor Constantine made Christianity the official religion of the Roman Empire, decided that they would like to dedicate their lives to God in a special way. They left the then-civilized world and headed to the desert (today the area of the Middle East) and lived either as hermits or in community. They flourished during the fourth and fifth centuries and they were the source of contemplative wisdom then and now.

Evagrius' deep psychological insight has made his articulation of prayer especially useful. He championed what he called pure prayer, a laying aside of all thoughts. Here is what he had to say:

> Stand guard over your spirit, keeping it free of concepts at the time of prayer, so that it may remain in its own deep calm. Thus God, who has compassion on the ignorant, will come to visit even such an insignificant person as yourself. That is when you will receive the most glorious gift of prayer. (*Chapters on Prayer,* No. 69)

At another place he said:

> Do not, by any means, try to fashion some image or visualize some form at the time of prayer. (Ibid., No. 114)

He is not throwing out all the other forms of prayer, but he says that there comes a time when this letting go should be part of our prayer. I hear his message coming through loud and clear. Don't "strive" or strain yourself to get a message, image, or an insight. They are important, but they can also be obstacles: go with the flow, open to the Spirit's workings.

I know people who leave retreats with headaches from trying too hard! Maybe our retreats should just be a resting in the Lord. After all, a lot of us are a bit more lovable when we are rested! Evagrius says elsewhere:

> Let me repeat this saying of mine . . . happy is the spirit that has attained to perfect formlessness at the time of prayer. . . . When you give yourselves to prayer, rise above every other joy. (Ibid., No. 117,153)

He is encouraging a prayer of resting, of being with the Lord, letting go of striving for words—in other words the apophatic approach. "Rise above every other joy." Sometimes when we pray and get what we don't want, we throw it back to God. It seems that we want the "payoff" immediately. We are looking for a sign or feeling that shows it is worthwhile to give time to prayer. But in reality, the "payoff" does not take place during the prayer time. The fruit of prayer is experienced in the activity of everyday life.

Evagrius was famous for something else, too. He was shrewd because he had a flair for what we today call psychology, which enabled him to present in an unusual, coherent, and pervasive form, the fruits of the tradition of self-knowledge. His writings show that out of this prayer of letting go of forms and concepts comes a remarkable amount of self-knowledge. He speaks of certain kinds of thoughts: "The monk's mind becomes befogged and besotted by these thoughts."

Evagrius sees these thoughts build around issues such as gluttony, fornication, love of money, depression, anger, listlessness, vainglory, and pride. They are known as the capital sins because they are at the roots of much of the confusion in our lives: a train of thoughts which engages the mind so that bit by bit, one drifts away from what one is supposed to be doing into a world of fantasy concerning ourselves. It is like a personal soap opera. We remember an incident, the details are before us, we build on the details and the next thing we know this story has taken on epic proportions. In fact when we are caught up in them, they befog the mind. Have we not heard ourselves say, "I can't even think straight?"

Thoughts are going to come up during our prayer time; if we do not let them go, they begin to control even our prayer. And so the letting go of thoughts in our prayer time helps us to be truly present to what we are about: to be in God's presence.

John Cassian (360–435) is one of the great pioneers in the early monastic world. St. Benedict, the father of Western monasticism, depended on his teaching in establishing the rule of Benedict. John Main, a Benedictine and popular teacher of the use of the Christian mantra prayer called "Christian Meditation," draws directly from the writings of John Cassian.

He was a wonderful writer and loved roaming around talking to the desert fathers and mothers and collecting many of the teachings of these marvelous people. He chose one particular man, Abba Isaac, to write extensively about. Here are some insights Abba Isaac, a desert hermit, shared with him.

> I must give you a formula for contemplation. If you carefully keep this formula before you and carefully learn to recollect it at all times, it will help you to mount to contemplation of high truth. Everyone who seeks continual recollection of God's presence uses this formula for meditation, intent on driving every other force

from his heart. You cannot keep this formula before you unless you are free from all bodily care. . . . [This means letting go of your usual concerns, it doesn't mean neglecting your physical health.] The formula is simply this: "O God, come to my assistance, O Lord, make haste to help me." (*Conferences,* 10.10)

That prayer, so familiar to those who pray the Liturgy of the Hours, came out of the desert fathers. So Cassian recommends the repetition of this verse:

I repeat, each one of you, whatever his condition in the spiritual life, needs to use this verse. Perhaps wandering thoughts surge about my soul like boiling water and I cannot control them. Nor can I pray without it being interrupted by silly images. I feel so dry that I am incapable of feeling spiritual feelings and many groans cannot save me from dreariness. I must needs say, "O God, come to my assistance, O Lord, make haste to help me." (Ibid.)

Here we see Cassian recommending a repetition of a phrase in order to let go of all else and be clear in one's intention to be with the Lord. He goes on to say:

Thus it attains the purest of prayers to which our earlier conferences lead, so far as the Lord deigns to grant this favor. [Notice he already knows it is not our own doing (acquired contemplation). We can only dispose ourselves and if God wishes to grant it, it will be granted (infused contemplation).] The prayer which looks for no visual image, uses neither words nor thoughts; the prayer therein, leaping up from a fire, the mind is rapt upwards, destitute of the aid of the senses, of any visible or material thing, pouring out its prayer to God. (Ibid.)

This is what receptive acquired contemplation is all about. A practice which expresses an intention that, if granted, leads to the gift of infused contemplation. So speaks Abba Isaac out of the desert, as recorded by John Cassian.

Pseudo-Dionysius (c. 500) is also important, not only for his own contribution, but he also seems to have had a powerful influence on the author of *The Cloud of Unknowing* (fourteenth century). I will discuss *The Cloud of Unknowing* in a later chapter. Let me share several of his writings. It is said of him that no writer has exerted more influence on Christian contemplation either in the East or the West. We don't know much about his background because he wrote anonymously. The closest guess we can make is that he was a Syrian monk of the sixth century. He writes:

> There is yet a higher way of knowing God. Besides the knowledge of God obtained by processes of philosophy and theology, these are processes of speculation, there is that most divine knowledge of God which takes place through ignorance. In this knowledge, the intellectual is illumined by the unsearchable depths of wisdom.

Knowledge such as this is not found in books nor obtained by human effort for it is a divine gift. We can prepare ourselves to receive it and this is done through prayer and purification. Here is Dionysius' advice.

> Do thou, then, in the inner practice of mystic contemplation, leave behind the senses and the operations of the intellect and all things that the senses or the intellect can perceive and all things which are not and things which are and strain upward to unknowing as far as may be toward the union with Him who is above all things and above all knowledge.

Leaving behind the senses, the operation of the intellect—in other words, thoughts, images, ideas, sense perceptions, memories, and so on—we are to "strain upward to unknowing," by which he means that desire to be with God which is beyond all our knowledge. It sounds awesome, but all he is saying is "rest" in the Lord.

John Climacus (d. 649) continues the apophatic approach with the following observations in the seventh century. Climacus was an abbot at a monastery at Mount Sinai. His famous work is *The Ladder of Divine Ascent.* On his ladder he had twenty-eight rungs! Don't worry: I will not cover all of them, but let me share this with you:

> Stillness is worshipping God unceasingly and waiting on Him. Let the remembrance of Jesus be present with your every breath. Then indeed you will appreciate the value of stillness. (*Paulist,* Step 27, 269–70)

> In your prayer there is no need for high-flown words, for it is the simple and unsophisticated babbling of children that have often won the hearts of the Father in heaven. Try not to talk excessively in your prayer, in case your mind is distracted by the search of

words. One word from the publican sufficed to placate God, and a single utterance saved the thief. Talkative prayer frequently distracts the mind and deludes it, whereas brevity makes for concentration. If it happens that as you pray, some words evoke delight and remorse within you, do not linger over it. (Step 28, 275–76)

When a man has found the Lord, he no longer has to use words when he is praying, for the Spirit Himself will intercede for him with groans than cannot be uttered (Rom 8:26) . . . do not form sensory images during prayer, for distractions will certainly follow. (Step 28, 279)

Once again we hear the affirmation of simplicity—no multiplication of words—a simple phrase or word. Multiplication of words can create distractions. Thoughts and the senses are very important in meditation, intercessory prayer, image prayer, and setting scenes for prayer, but in this particular prayer of receptive acquired contemplation that moves into infused contemplation, they are let go of at this particular time. We need to trust that the Holy Spirit will recall to our minds what we need to remember.

After John Climacus, we don't have much writing on the subject available for the next five hundred years. The apophatic tradition survived, at least in seminal form until the twelfth century. William of St. Thierry (d. 1148) is our next important author. Here's what he had to say in his little treatise on prayer:

If I envision for you, my God, any form whatever, or anything that has a form, I place myself in idolatry. . . . Rid yourselves of all the usual ideas about locality and place and get a firm hold of this. You have found God in yourself. . . . What is more certain, more dependable than this by which our intention may orient itself and which our affections may lay hold?" (*On Prayer*)

Here we have William of St. Thierry emphasizing, "You have found God in yourself." We should rid ourselves of the usual ideas about prayer. And in another place he speaks of our tendency to cling to our sense perceptions of Jesus:

But again, sometimes in our prayer, we clasp the feet of Jesus, holding on for dear life. We are attracted to the human form of the Son of God, develop a sort of bodily devotion, we do not err. Yet, in so doing, we retard and hinder spiritual prayer. He Himself tells us, "It is expedient for you that I go away. If I do not go away, the Paraclete will not come to you." (Ibid.)

Christ doesn't exist any longer in bodily form as we understand it. Mary Magdalene learned it when she head the words from Jesus, "Don't touch me." He didn't want her to become attached to her perceptions of His body. He has risen. We, too, deal with the risen Lord and with the Spirit moving in us and touching us. If we get too attached, it could be a form of idolatry.

When we ask people to sit in silence, they sometimes say, "I have to picture myself sitting with Christ." That's not Christ they are picturing. That's their own image. It is all right to do this to get us started and in the mood, but finally we have to let that image go for a time. We can be limited by our impression of who Christ is. For instance, if our impression is that of sweet, meek, and gentle Jesus, then we distort Jesus because He is that and much more. Or if our image of Jesus is the one who demands obedience and punishes, He is that but much more.

William of St. Thierry comments here on the gift of infused contemplation:

> But this way of thinking about God does not lie at the disposal of the thinker. It is a gift of grace. It is bestowed by the Holy Spirit who breathes where He chooses, when He chooses, how He chooses and upon whom He chooses. Our part is to continually prepare our hearts by ridding our will of foreign attachments, our reason and intellect of anxieties, our memories of idleness and absorbing thoughts, sometimes even of necessary business. In God's good time, when God sees fit, at the sound of the Holy Spirit's breathing, the elements which constitute thought may be free at once to come together and do their work, each contributing its share of the outcome of joy for the heart. (*Golden Epistle*)

This will displays pure affection for the joy which the Lord gives. The memory yields faithful material; the intellect affords the sweetness of experience. What can we do to have this happen? Simply prepare ourselves. Dispose ourselves. We say, "Here I am Lord; do what you need to do. I'm open to the Holy Spirit's work in my life. Be it done unto me according to your word."

God sees our willingness to consent. We are like a bird standing on the branch of a tree, with our wings out, waiting for the slightest breeze, or like the eagle riding the air currents to carry us to wherever we need to be. The interesting thing in this prayer is that we don't know when it happens.

I think it is worthwhile to read William of St. Thierry's comment again. It is one of the clearest statements concerning infused contemplation and our part in the preparation for the gift.

Before we move on I would like to comment on a concern that some have about thoughts and insights that are received during the prayer time. William refers to this concern in the last quote. Any insights, thoughts, or solutions that come up during the prayer will be remembered after the prayer is over if they are important, even though we let go of them during the prayer itself.

Bernard of Clairveaux (1080–1153), our next superstar, has some similar thoughts:

> Frequent needs make it necessary to call upon God often, to taste by frequent contact and to discover by tasting how sweet the Lord is. It is in this way, the taste of His own sweetness leads us to love God in purity more than our need alone which prompts us to do so. The Samaritans set us an example. When they said to the woman who told them the Lord was there "Now we believe, not because of your words but because we have heard Him for ourselves and we know that truly He is the savior of the world." In the same way, I urge you, let us follow their example and rightly say to our human nature, "Now we love God not because He meets our needs, but we have tasted and we know how sweet the Lord is."

Bernard's main concern is that sometimes we just go to God for what we need rather than go to God for God's sake only. A marvelous example can be given from a marriage when one asks their partner, "Do you love me because of me? Or because of what I do for you?" If the love is based on loving the other for his or her sake, then there is a commitment to the person as person and not to the person as doer. Bernard is saying that sweetness comes, as when the people said to the Samaritan woman, "Now we believe, not because of your words, or nice feelings or images, but because we have heard and experienced Him for ourselves. We know that truly He is the savior."

The Flemish mystic, Jan van Ruysbroeck (1293–1381) is relatively unknown, but he is my favorite. He writes eloquently of God's free gift of calling all who are open to union with him:

> Now understand the free work of our Lord which He works in everyone who is open to them. The first of these, which God works in all persons in common, is that He calls and invites them all to union with Him. (*The Spiritual Espousals and Other Works,* 161)

And this is how the union and resting is maintained:

> There we will abide—unified, empty, imageless—raised up through love to the open bareness of our minds, for when we transcend all things in love and die to all rational observations in a dark state of unknowing, we become transformed through the working of the Eternal Word, who is an image of the Father. . . . What we are is what we see, and what we see is what we are, for our mind, our life, our very being are raised up in a state of oneness and united with the truth which is God Himself. (Ibid., 171)

Here are some additional insights into the prayer:

> There are three other things which are higher and which give a person a firm foundation and render him capable of enjoying and experiencing God whenever he wishes. The first of these is to rest in Him whom one enjoys. This takes place when the lover is overcome and obsessed by his Beloved in bare essential love. Here the lover is lovingly immersed in his Beloved, so that each is entirely the other's, both in possession and in rest. There follows the second thing, which is called falling asleep in God. This occurs when the spirit sinks away from itself without knowing how or where this takes place. Then there follows the third and last thing which can be expressed in words. It takes place when the spirit sees a darkness which it cannot enter by means of the power of reason. In this state a person feels that he has died and lost his way and that he has become one with God, without difference. When he feels himself to be one with God, then God Himself is his peace, his enjoyment and his rest. (Ibid., 183)

He spells out the three ways of experiencing God: first, to rest in Him whom one enjoys; second, to fall asleep in God; third, to be one with God beyond our own powers, through the Holy Spirit. Contained here are all the levels of contemplation.

Julian of Norwich (d. 1416), whose contribution to the apophatic tradition is the ability of allowing us to consider God beyond our ordinary preconceived notions, brings in the concept of the Mother:

> As truly as God is Our Father, so truly is God Our Mother. And He revealed this in everything, especially in these sweet words when He said, "I am He." That is to say, I am He, the power and the goodness of Fatherhood. I am He, the wisdom and lovingness of Mother-hood. I am He, the life and grace which is all blessed love. I am He, the Trinity. I am He, the unity. I am He, the supreme goodness of every kind of thing. I am He who makes you to love. I am He who makes you to long. I am He the endless fulfillment of all true desire. (*Showings*)

The beauty of what is offered here is the concept of motherhood. And the motherhood role is given primarily to Jesus! She writes later on:

> Jesus, our mother, is our true mother in nature by our first creation. He is our true mother in grace by his taking our created nature. All the loving works and all the sweet loving offices of beloved motherhood are appropriate to the second person of the Blessed Trinity. (Ibid.)

Jesus became a human being, a man. But Jesus as risen and glorified is no longer just man. Jesus is glorified. The beauty of this concept is that Julian helps us to go beyond the concepts. We look upon Jesus as having the characteristics of mother as Julian expresses it. I have trouble not making God male, as does much of the church. How do we do that? If I'm really talking about God, I go beyond male/female. Julian enables us to think beyond preconceived concepts so we can approach Jesus as glorified. There is always the chance that this will be misunderstood. I realize that. But if God is infinite, then any term limits God. Or better, words help define God, but in the end all words are inadequate as we enter into the mystery of God.

Now let's turn to St. Teresa of Ávila (1515–82). To capture the gusto of her writing, we really should go to the Spanish text.

It's so earthy, vital, and immediate. Most spiritual guides are much less intense and passionate about prayer than she was. She writes:

> The soul is doubtful as to what has really happened until it has had a good deal of experience of it. It wonders if the whole thing were your imagination. Or if it has been asleep. If the favor was a gift of God or if the devil was transfigured into an angel of light as you sit quietly. Is it God? How can I be sure it is God? Maybe it's the devil. It retains a thousand misgivings. What are you doing? What are you doing sitting here quiet? Shouldn't you be doing something? Agile little lizards will try to slip in! They can do no harm, especially if we take no notice of them. Let them come, let them go. These are the thoughts that proceed from imagination. From what has been said, it will be seen that they are often very troublesome. (*Interior Castle*)

When we sit quietly, our thoughts and anxieties are going to attempt to take over. First of all, we'll start wondering if this is just our imagination. Did we experience God or did we not? Maybe it's the devil. Maybe a feeling that we're not worthy to just sit here. We have to arrive at a certain place to just sit quietly with our God. That's when the little lizards come around. We've already experienced some of this. In the ten minutes we take before each chapter we can find lizards! Our minds never stop. If we attack the lizards, then the lizards control us! We can spend our entire prayer time just stomping on lizards. It is impossible not to have thoughts and images spring up in our mind. If we try to "not have" thoughts, we will be doomed to failure. We must be able to let thoughts go as soon as they come. They, like the lizards, move away as rapidly as they move toward us if we pay little attention to them. We just let them go. Teresa's image captures the problem and the solution quite vividly:

> It is well to seek greater solitude so as to make room for the Lord and allow His majesty to do His own work in us. The most we should do is occasionally and quite gently to utter a single word. Like a person giving a little puff to a candle when he sees it has almost gone out so as to make it burn again. Though, if it were fully alight, I suppose the only result would be to put it out. (*Way of Perfection*)

We use the word only to keep the flame going. If we concentrate on the word, it is like concentrating on blowing and the candle will go out. Another way of putting it is that if we concentrate on the blowing, we begin to forget about the light of the candle. Teresa continues: "I think the puff should be a gentle one. If we begin to tax our brains making long speeches, the will may become active again" (Ibid).

Our brain loves to analyze. Check posture, check foot position, how about the breathing? We can go on indefinitely:

> So when the will finds itself in this state of quiet, it must take no more notice of the understanding than it would of a madman. For if it tries to draw the understanding along with itself, it is bound to grow preoccupied and restless with the result that this state of prayer will be all effort and no gain and the soul will lose what God has been giving it without any effort on its own. (Ibid.)

Did you ever have a party where everything is going along smoothly and everyone is having a great time, but suddenly you begin to worry and fret? So you start to push, and try very hard to make everyone have a good time? When they are already having a good time? You can end up ruining the party. You're working hard and perhaps feeling good about yourself for stirring up things your way, but everyone else is murmuring about the person who could not just relax, be, and simply enjoy the party. Listen to Teresa on "relaxing" in prayer:

> Pay great attention to the following comparison which the Lord suggested to me when I was in a state of prayer which seems to me very appropriate. The soul is like an infant still at its mother's breast. Such is the mother's care for it that she gives it milk without it having to ask for it, doing no more than moving its lips. This is what happens here. The will simply loves and no effort needs to be made by the understanding. For it is the Lord's pleasure, that without exercising its thought, the soul should realize that it is in His company. So when we enter into prayer, we believe we are in God's company, and simply drink the milk which His majesty puts into our mouth and enjoy its sweetness. The Lord desires it to know that it is He who is granting it that favor and that in its enjoyment of it He too rejoices. But it is not His will that the soul try to understand how it is enjoying it. (Ibid.)

It reminds me of the wonderful story Catherine Dougherty de Hueck tells of a priest who came to her retreat center in Canada. He was heading for one of the hermitages where he intended to spend two weeks in prayer and solitude. As she looked out her window she saw him heading toward the hermitage with a large attaché case. She ran out after him and demanded to see what was in the case. He opened it and there was his Bible, Liturgy of the Hours prayer book, other spiritual reading books, a few tapes, a tape recorder, a Walkman radio to check the news each day, some papers, and other assorted stuff. She could not believe her eyes. She took the Bible out and handed it to the priest. She closed the attaché case with the rest of the stuff. She scolded him, "When a man goes on his honeymoon, he doesn't bring a manual!" Two weeks later she returned his attaché case.

When we go to God, who needs to figure out what is happening? It will just happen. Teresa goes on:

> It is not His will that the soul try to understand how it is enjoying this and what it is that it is enjoying. It should lose all thought of itself. He who is at its side will not fail to see what is best for it. If it begins to strive with its mind so that the mind may be appraised of what is happening and is thus induced to share in it, it will be quite unable to do so and the soul will lose the milk and forego the divine substance. (Ibid.)

If we are not careful we will start drinking our own concoction, our preconceived ideas and plans, instead of the milk of God. That can be pretty boring. I like the term, "spiritual cannibalism." We go into prayer; we consume our ideas, thoughts, and images; we eat ourselves up. We don't come out refreshed. We come out spiritually fatigued. Remember it is not our task to fit God into our lives, but to fit ourselves into God's life. When we try to fit God into our lives the image that comes to my mind is someone who has a salt-water swimming pool and believes he has captured the ocean. Notice who is in control. But when we fit ourselves into God's life, then the image is the ocean itself. There is a big difference between a pool and the ocean. Which direction are we going—fitting God into our life or fitting ourselves into God's life? The direction makes all the difference.

Teresa's good friend, John of the Cross (1542–91), had good things to say also. He was a poet. Teresa was an older woman by the time she befriended John, and she was of an entirely different temperament. They had a close relationship. John has this to say about prayer:

> The attitude necessary in the Night of Sense is to pay no attention to discursive meditation, since it is not the time for it. They should allow the soul to remain in rest and in quietude, even though it may seem very obvious to them that they are doing nothing and wasting time. (*Dark Night of the Soul,* chap. 10)

> Seek in reading and you will find in meditation, knock in prayer and it will be opened to you in contemplation. (*Maxims and Counsels*)

> What we need most in order to make progress is to be silent before this great Good with our appetites and tongue, for the language He best hears is silent love. (Ibid.)

> A person should not bear attachment to anything, neither to the practice of meditation nor to any savoring of sensory or spiritual goods nor to any other apprehensions. He should be very free and annihilate it, regarding all these things. Because any thought, or discursive reflection or satisfaction upon which he may want to lean would impede and disquiet him. It would make noise in the profound silence of his senses and his spirit, which he possesses for the sake of this deep and delicate listening. (*The Living Flame of Love,* stanza 3)

There is much more I could quote from St. John, but I am sure you are getting the idea about receptive acquired contemplation. John's comments are very much in tune with the spiritual writers before him.

From the time of Julian of Norwich in 1416 until 1751 a number of things happened in our prayer tradition. The Roman Catholic Church after the Council of Trent emerged from the Reformation of the sixteenth century with new anxieties and certitudes. It was a church of the necessity of law, order, and piety. Prayer was schematized with disciplines and spiritual exercises proper to each stage.

In spirituality people felt more confident with certain well-mapped devotional exercises like spiritual reading and visits to

the Blessed Sacrament. When it came to mental prayer, they pre-
ferred an orderly succession of points, resolutions, and acts of
self-examination. Anything beyond this process was questionable. Natural and supernatural were segregated, and strict
requirements controlled admission into contemplative prayer.

No doubt many people were well-nourished by the prevailing
piety with its defined systems. Forms of prayer such as contemplation were reserved for the people who were advanced on the spiritual journey, and this did not include the ordinary people in the
pews. No doubt, this portrayal is something of a caricature of this
period of history, but I believe that era set forth a common mindset
and attitude that has carried over, even today. I know people who
have gone for spiritual direction, feeling called to contemplation,
and have been told they were filled with pride to think that. And yet
our tradition speaks of this desire for contemplation, as being part
of the ordinary prayer development of faithful followers of Christ.

We are gradually seeing the development of a new kind of
spiritual director who is open to the simpler way of prayer and
who is not bound by formats. The simpler way is one that is
receptive and apophatic in its approach. Again, this is not to deny
the need for the kataphatic. We need both orientations in our
spiritual tradition, but there must be freedom in our response to
God's call to prayer.

St. Francis de Sales (1567–1622) is the classic example of the
mindset prevailing after the Council of Trent. As I mentioned
above, prayer was schematized with disciplines and spiritual exercises proper to each stage. He was a fine spiritual master, a bishop,
a director of souls, and a man involved with social action. In his
Introduction to the Devout Life, he presented a way to meditate:

1. Preparation: You place yourself in the presence of God, pray for
   assistance, compose the place, and imagine a scene from the life
   of Jesus.
2. Considerations: Identify those images in the scene that affect
   you.
3. Affections and Resolutions: Convert feelings into understanding
   and then into resolutions.
4. Acts of the Will: Pray for the strength to carry out these resolutions.

5. Conclusion: Thanksgiving, oblation (offering the results of the meditation), petitions to fulfill in your life this day
6. Spiritual Nosegay: That Scripture phrase, image or idea you carry through the day with you from this meditation.

This form of meditation is very powerful and beneficial but often it ended with step four. Prayer was never meant to end with a resolution leading to action. Prayer is relational and strives not only toward responsibility but also intimacy with God. Resolutions are part of the intimacy but not the end product which this type of prayer seems to imply. Retreats were never meant to be only times of resolving problems and just making resolutions, but a time of intimacy with our God.

For much of our own century, learning to pray took this form in school: say your prayers, think about what you are saying, and then make a resolution to live a good life. There is nothing wrong with this approach to prayer, but there is more to prayer than just this. The movement toward resting with God, or simply being with God, is missing from the "formula." I will explore this aspect later in the book.

The format we have been discussing was part of my own seminary training in the 1950s. We would gather in the chapel early in the morning. The points of meditation according to de Sales were either read to us, or we read from our own books during the twenty minutes of meditation. All three hundred of us began the meditation kneeling. After a while, it became a contest, and it seemed the measure of holiness was to see who could kneel the longest.

Please don't get me wrong. This is a fine exercise, but when kneeling is made a measure of interior holiness, I have some reservations. If that mindset ever returns I will invent a belt, like the one window cleaners use and place it on the back of the pew in front of us. We can strap ourselves in and adjust the strap so that we are kneeling up straight and then we can all look holy together. It would be quite a sight—what do you think? Not a good idea? Then let it go ever so gently.

Our next spiritual guide, Jean de Caussade (d. 1751), reacted to the approach to prayer as outlined by de Sales. He found some fault with it. We have a collection of his talks and writings. His major work is called *Abandonment to Divine Providence*.

He knew very well that it was normal for spiritual writers of the time to dwell at length on the dangers of the illusion that a person might think he or she was worthy of praying the contemplative way. These writers feared that many persons who were serious about leading a spiritual life would fall into the illusion that they were called to a contemplative way of prayer. The writers of that time believed that this was an "elite" calling reserved for very few. "What makes you think that you're better than someone else?" But against this allegation that it was dangerous to go beyond the discipline of the routine of conventional piety, with all its works and exercises, Jean de Caussade indicated that it might be dangerous *not* to abandon it.

In his letter to a nun, he warns against being enslaved by devotional practices, bodily or interior:

> Believe me, you have too many practices already. What is needed is rather a progressive inner simplification. Too many people identify spiritual prowess with being perpetually busy heaping meditation upon meditation, prayer upon prayer, reading upon reading instead of learning from the simple souls the great secret of knowing how, from time to time, to hold yourself back a little in peace and silence, attentive before God. (*Letters*)

As de Caussade points out, this mistake leads to unnecessary discouragement on the part of those who are not good at this kind of "hectic" piety. Worse still, it encourages people to place their trust in their own good works. By multiplying these good works and devotions, people think that God is more apt to do something for them. They substitute these for the mercy of God and the merits of Christ. To be wrapped up in hectic piety could stem from simple self-love and pride. We can become as dangerously attached to our own will in matters of piety and even holiness as we can in worldly things. De Caussade pinpoints this quite well:

> And such pious pig-headedness is still self-love, regardless of how spiritualized. Nothing is more contrary to the spirit of God than this kind of hidden unconscious vanity which makes us rely more

on our own insights and resolutions and will power than on God's grace. All of which lures us, unaware, into telling ourselves, complacently, how much we are doing for God, for our salvation and for our perfection. (*Prayer of the Heart*)

It's insidious. Notice what he stresses. He says this doing for God and over relying on ourselves is unconscious vanity. He's not talking about something deliberate or malicious. He never tires of reminding us that much of what God does in us, He does without our knowledge.

How cherished you are without realizing it. What great things God is bringing to pass in you, all the more securely because the manner of it is so dark, so unknown. Oh, my God, it is our weakness, our wretched self-pride, our pride that reduces us to be unable to do great things in us by hiding in us and working as it were, behind our backs, for fear that we should corrupt your gifts by appropriating them to ourselves by vain secret complacency. (*Letters*)

Oh, how happy we are without knowing it! There's an inner happiness that comes from cutting loose of that attachment to have to know everything. There we have the whole mystery of this hidden way in which God leads us. Go back to Gregory of Nyssa and the image of wanting to see God's face and getting only to see God's back.

I know that in my spiritual counseling, done primarily at parish missions and retreats, a large number of people judge their lives as drifting from God because they do not see how God is working in their lives or because they don't feel God's presence. How do we feel God's presence? Many of the feelings that we call the presence of God are nice warm fuzzies, really. When the expectation is present that a sign of God's presence is warm fuzzies, then the relationship with God has deteriorated, for it is then based on feeling rather than faith.

So de Caussade really began to go against the trend in the eighteenth century. Very few listened, but now, he has become one of the masters to whom we turn.

We are still suffering from the syndrome he tried to undo. We still have a busy, cluttered, hectic piety without much insight into how we might simplify our lives or our piety. This is the context into which Teresa and John had to try to talk about their kind of prayer life. You can understand why they had a difficult time of it. And no wonder everyone loved Francis de Sales. He spoke to his times. What he said was clear, orderly, systematic. People knew exactly where they stood, but that's not what constitutes the spiritual journey. The only certitude in the spiritual journey is that we are passionately loved by God and God wants to be passionately loved in returned. Everything else is negotiable, and anything can be a surprise.

Thérèse of Lisieux (1873–97) lived her "little way," doing the simple things to perfection. Her vocation was to fill each moment with total and radical self-emptying love and thereby to embrace all. Thérèse's greatness comes from her living out of her favorite quotation from St. John of the Cross, "Love is repaid by love alone." To desire and to succeed in filling each moment with perfect love is not a "little way" but the full flowering of Christian life. Thus her life exemplified those qualities of surrender and of detachment cultivated by contemplative prayer: I must decrease; God must increase.

> I wanted to find an elevator which would raise me to Jesus, for I am too small to climb the rough stairway of perfection. I searched then in the scriptures for some sign of this elevator, the object of my desires, and I read these words coming from the mouth of Eternal Wisdom: "Whoever is a little one, let him come to me" (Prv 9:4). . . . "As one who a mother caresses, so I will comfort you; you shall be carried at the breast, and upon the knees they shall caress you" (Is 66:13,12). . . . The elevator which must raise me to heaven is your arms, O Jesus. And for this I have no need to grow up, but rather I had to remain little and become this more and more. (*Story of a Soul,* chap. 10)

The simpler the prayer the better:

> How great is the power of prayer! . . . To be heard it is not necessary to read from a book some beautiful formula composed for the occasion. . . . Outside the Divine Office which I am very unworthy to recite, I do not have the courage to force myself to search out beautiful prayers in books . . . it really gives me a headache. . . . I say very simply to God what I wish to say . . . and He always understands me. For me, prayer is an aspiration of the heart, it is

a simple glance directed to heaven, it is a cry of gratitude and love in the midst of trail as well as joy; finally, it is something great, supernatural, which expands my soul and unites me to Jesus. (Ibid., chap.11)

Last but not least among our superstars, we will introduce here our contemporary, Thomas Merton (1915–68). Merton was a Trappist monk and thirty years after his death his writings are still in demand. Of extraordinary importance is a letter he sent to a Sufi scholar named Abdul Aziz. Sufis are the mystics of the Moslem tradition, and when Aziz would ask Merton about his own prayer life, he would evade the question, but Aziz was persistent and finally we have a precious letter that Merton sent him. Here is an excerpt from his letter:

Now you ask about my method of meditation. Simply speaking, I have a very simple way of prayer. It is centered entirely on the presence of God and to His will and His love. That is to say, it is centered on Faith by which alone we can know the presence of God. One might say this gives my meditation the character described by the Prophet (Mohammad) as being before God as if you saw him. Yet it does not mean imagining anything or conceiving a precious image of God. To my mind, this would be a form of idolatry. On the contrary it is a manner of adoring Him as all. There is in my heart this great thirst to recognize the nothingness of all that is not God. My prayer then, is a kind of praise, rising up out of the center of nothingness and silence. If I am still present myself, I recognize this as an obstacle. If He wills, He can then make the nothingness into a total clarity. If He does not will, then the nothingness actually seems to itself to be an object and remains an obstacle. Such is my ordinary way of prayer. It is not thinking about anything but a direct seeking of the face of the invisible which cannot be found unless we become lost in Him who is invisible. (*Thomas Merton, Brother Monk*, Basil Pennington)

This is a very rare piece explaining Merton's prayer. It captures the apophatic approach and what we have called receptive acquired contemplation. Centering Prayer got its name from some of Merton's statements which implied we should pray out of the center of our being—particularly that phrase in his letter to Aziz —"My prayer then, is a kind of praise, rising up out of the center of nothingness and silence." When Merton lived in his hermitage, we do know that he spent about three hours a day in this kind of prayer. All his writing came out of his silence. He felt that any writing about contemplation that did not come out of silence was prone to be ego-invested. All the writing that came out of silence had the spirit of God behind it. So before he picked up his pen, he spent time in silence.

I thank you for the opportunity to share these great writers with you. There were many others that I could have mentioned, such as Augustine of Hippo, Dom Augustine Baker, Benedict of Nursia, Pierre de Berulle, Catherine of Siena, Dom John Chapman, Jeanne de Chantal, Pierre Teilhard de Chardin, Gregory the Great, Hildegarde of Bingen, Walter Hilton, Richard Rolle, Ignatius of Loyola, Dom Vital Lehodey, Mechtilde of Magdeburg, Meister Eckhart, and John Tauler. Not to mention some of today's popular writers.

I wanted to share with you my favorites and those that supported the apophatic tradition—in other words the rest of the story. In the following chapters I will be discussing the writings of Guigo (+1188) in regard to *lectio divina* and *The Cloud of Unknowing* as one of the foundations to Centering Prayer.

Let's listen once again to:

Gregory of Nyssa: Prayer is a deep yearning for intimacy with God and we find that God will dictate the terms of the prayer relationship.

Evagrius: There is a call to let go of concepts, images and ideas. If we are not able to do that then the mind becomes befogged and full of distractions.

John Cassian: Keep the prayer to a single phrase or word such as "O God come to my assistance. O Lord make haste to help me."

Pseudo-Dionysius: There is a level of relationship with God in prayer which comes out of unknowing. What is meant by this is that we come to know God on God's terms rather than ours. Our mind is illuminated through the fidelity of prayer.

John Climacus: Let us not under estimate the power of a single word or phrase in prayer, think of the example of the publican and the prodigal son.

William of St. Thierry: An attachment to the image of God in prayer can be a form of idolatry. Don't hold on to it; be open to the spirit praying us.

Bernard of Clairveaux: Go to God for God's sake not just for our needs. Taste and see how sweet the Lord can be.

Jan van Ruysbroeck: The three ways of experiencing God: first, to rest in Him whom one enjoys; second, to fall asleep in God; third, to be one with God beyond our own powers, through the Holy Spirit.

Julian of Norwich: In calling God "Mother" we are moved beyond the finiteness of terms to the infinite—going beyond our preconceived notions of God.

Teresa of Ávila: Confront the thoughts and the experience of silence and the power of a single prayer word prayed gently.

John of the Cross: The power of silence, the letting go of thoughts, and resting in the Lord are keys to prayer and our transformation.

Francis de Sales: Lets us see the power of the kataphatic method of prayer, which should never be neglected but should also move us toward the apophatic.

Jean de Caussade: One can become perpetually busy in prayer—the need to be open to a simplification of our prayer. He also comments on our need to let go of wanting to know what God is doing in our lives, to just experience it, and let it unfold.

Thérèse of Lisieux: The "little way" of consenting to God and the move away from the wordiness of prayer to a simpler prayer method.

Thomas Merton: The term, "Centering Prayer" was drawn from his writings. In sharing his prayer practice he described it as a prayer of resting in one's center where God dwells.

In the beginning, I state that as part of dealing with the fundamentals of Centering Prayer it is important to look at the Christian contemplative tradition. I have selected a few "superstars" that

I feel are important in developing the apophatic approach to prayer (receptive acquired contemplation) which leads to the gift of infused contemplation. I believe that Centering Prayer comes out of this apophatic tradition.

Please take the time to read them more fully and prayerfully. They will not disappoint you.

3 ❈

Spirituality and the Spiritual Journey

I look forward to sharing some further thoughts about the topic of spirituality and the spiritual journey. I invite you to reread what I presented concerning the spiritual journey, spirituality, spiritual exercises, and prayer itself in the first chapter. There are some additional points which I would like to make.

On this journey we are supported by a number of teachings which I believe are the foundation of our discussion. The first is the doctrine of the Trinity. This doctrine is intrinsic to our faith, and it structures our prayer life. At the very heart of the Godhead is relationship—the dynamic interplay between Father, Son, and Holy Spirit—Creator, Redeemer, and Sanctifier. We need to be aware that the Trinity abides within us and it is that dynamic that transforms us. Baptism is the first great public celebration of this indwelling, but we also understand that the Trinity dwells in every person, baptized or not. The fullness of baptism doesn't happen all of a sudden. It is the public celebration of what is invisibly real in every person and develops throughout the years as we open ourselves and respond more and more to that presence within us. It incorporates us into the community that celebrates that presence; we acknowledge that presence in all.

We were taught that God is everywhere. We all take that for granted. We don't say God is everywhere with a few exceptions. We begin with this simple truth: God is everywhere and in everything. Consequences flow from this belief, especially when it is examined thoughtfully. The presence of the Trinity within us means that our journey is defined as relational from the beginning. We interact with God within us.

Relational considerations don't stop there. The indwelling of the Trinity means also that our spiritual journey is worked out in relationships with other people. We are born into a family, live in a particular area, work in a specific place, deal with the same people day in and day out. Many of the people in our lives are a help to us. We truly appreciate their presence. But there are times when we feel that we are living and working with the wrong people. They are not making life easy for us. We could live our lives much better if we were with different, more mature people. Alas, the truth is more likely that we need to be with the people we are with because these are the people who know how to "push the buttons" we need pushed. These buttons are pushed so we can become who we are supposed to be. We are, thank God, stuck with these people. It is with these people and these relationships that the Spirit speaks to us. I have no confirmed message that God has spoken directly to me on a personal level (yet!), but I know God has spoken to me through the people in my life.

I have a friend who always likes to say, "I could be a saint if it weren't for people." And I always say, "You will be a saint *because* of the people in your life." He then looks at me and tells me that the only reason I say that is because I don't have to live with these people.

It helps at times to realize we are not "gifts" to live with either. We might meditate on the fact that other people are stuck with us, too. We're no prize packages at times and our flaws are what push other's buttons to further their spiritual growth. Fortunately for their spirituality, we have lots of flaws.

By the way, if you think you are "perfect," I have an antidote for that. Just talk to four of your best friends. Begin an ordinary conversation with them. After your friends have been talking for a while, ask them if there are any little things you do that cause a small amount of abrasion, annoyance, irritation, or downright outrage? At this point, begin to take notes—casually at first, then at greater speed and in more detail. After these notes are typed up and ordered a bit, they can become a spiritual agenda to be dealt with for the rest of your life. This isn't a pleasant assignment, it is more like radical surgery on one's vanity. On second thought, maybe we'd better not do this. Take my word for it: we are not perfect. Thank God people are generous and loving enough to put up with us.

We can't run away from people and events. Unfinished business will always be there for us to deal with. Too many times when we're having difficulties with people or a serious challenge arises, we don't want to face up to it. We decide not to resolve the difficulty. It never goes away on its own. Real growth takes place working the unfinished business out, no matter how difficult it may be.

We even do that with God. We say for example, "Because I am sick so often, I have stopped believing in God. If God were real and present in my life, I wouldn't be sick." Those are our terms. "God better conform to our rules. People have to, so does God. Who needs God anyway?" Our notion of relationship structures our spiritual journey, from the exalted belief in the Trinity to our daily interactions. St. John, in his Epistle, talks about how can you love the God you do not see, if you do not love those you do see. The relational factor is of great importance on this journey.

Besides our belief in the Trinity, we believe in Jesus and His Incarnation. Our journey is either incarnational or it is not Christian. Jesus became a human being and lived a human existence with all that entails. Jesus was paving the way for us. He was setting an example for us. He never denied His humanity, He celebrated it. The more we appreciate our humanity, the more we discover God in the human. There is no running away from humanity. We were never called to be angels. We are body, mind, and spirit. The events in life keep reminding us how human we are. Thank God.

Recently in my reading I came across a quote—I can't remember the source—which touched me deeply on this topic of our humanity. "We were born spiritual and we spend the rest of our lives dealing with our humanity." What an interesting way of viewing life. It doesn't sound correct at first but when you think about it, it puts everything in a different perspective. I have recently been bonding with a baby boy by the name of Austin Anthony. Not having my own children, I have found throughout the years that certain little ones come along and have an impact on my life. When I am holding him in my arms I have a real sense of the presence of God—that is, if he is playing or sleeping; I am not sure what I sense when he does not want to stop crying. The point is how powerful God's presence is in the little one. Have you not experienced the same thing?

We have been a thought in the mind of God since the beginning of time. Our God has been communicating with us for millions of years. Then we were conceived and this thought of God's became enfleshed and our Passover (years on earth) began. It is our human condition that we deal with—this is where all the challenges take place. Let me give you an example. Have you ever noticed what happens when some people try to be spiritual? They act strange: they think they have to act in a way different than before to such an extent that they start to get out of touch with reality and begin to act like angels, or rather as if they are above others. Well, thank God, that only lasts during the honeymoon period of their conversion. They settle back finally realizing that they are only human after all. There is nothing wrong with honeymoons, but who has the energy to keep on that emotional high for the rest of life? Finally we come back to earth and really live life. God never allows us to forget our humanity.

The problem in trying to be human on our spiritual journey is our desire for neatness. We want everything to fit together. Although the spiritual journey has many characteristics, neatness is not one of them. Life isn't neat, let alone fair. There are times when even the spiritual journey itself does not seem fair.

Pat Livingston, a single parent who used to give workshops for separated and divorced people, tells a wonderful story about her son. He was in Little League. He never could get a hit. His best effort was a walk. No matter how he swung, he never got a hit. One day a miracle happened. He swung with his usual gusto, but this time he hit the ball, and he actually hit a home run. He ran around all the bases, and everyone was yelling and cheering as he touched home base. However, the umpire called him out because he missed first base! He kept a stiff upper lip. On the way home, he started to cry. "Why, Mom? Why, Mom?" And all his mother could say to him was "Life isn't fair." Pat knew first-hand what she was talking about and she shared that wisdom with her son: Life is life. We try to make it fair, just, honest, good, neat, and happy. And we get exhausted making it fair and just and honest and all the rest, rather than just living life. Life is messy. We'll never get it neat. Remember, nothing grows in sterile soil.

Let me tell you another story about some parishioners in Colorado who insisted that they wanted flowers in front of the church no matter what. Every time they planted them, deer and elk would come by and eat them. Finally they resolved the problem. They now have a wonderful display of wooden flowers on the front lawn of the church. The flowers seem wonderful, waving in the breeze on their wire stems. The parishioners just have to wash them off once in a while and they are fine. They are always the same, destined never to grow and above all never to cause a mess. But what was lost in the translation?

The Incarnation reminds us that the spiritual journey is a human one. Jesus had to deal with His humanity and He set an example for us. Just think of the various events of His life: His birth, His growing up, teaching in the temple at an early age, and having to take over the family business after the death of Joseph. Consider His public life: Cana, conflicts with the Jewish leaders, resolving difficulties among the Apostles, preaching to the people and then His arrest, trial, death, and resurrection. Quite a bit to think about? Jesus was not able to get away from His humanity, nor did He want to, because it was important to His mission. We are not going to get away from our humanity; it keeps coming back to remind us that we are far from being angels.

Some who read Scripture say that the flesh is evil and a detriment to the journey. We read the Scriptures wrongly when we read "flesh" as human nature. The term used there means flesh gone wild—not used properly. Since God loved our humanity so much that Jesus became human, why do we deny the beauty of what God took as an instrument of revelation? Our humanity gets a little crazy at times and it always will. We are disciples, not the Messiah, with no claim on always being perfect.

Besides our belief in the Trinity and the Incarnation we learn from Jesus that human life has seasons. These seasons are called the Paschal Mystery. The Paschal Mystery is a liturgical term which represents the events that we celebrate during Holy Week. Our Lord experienced Palm Sunday, Holy Thursday, Good Friday, Holy Saturday, and Easter Sunday. All that Jesus said about "doing the will of the Father" is fulfilled in the Paschal Mystery. There was no way in which He could leap from Palm Sunday to Easter. He asked the Father not to make Him drink the cup but the Father's answer was, "you must" and He did. He had already lived through His Palm Sunday and Holy Thursday experience. Now, after His Father said He had to drink the cup, He experienced the cross on Good Friday, the separation on Holy Saturday, and then the triumph of Easter.

Jesus revealed a lot about humanity and His life in the seasons of the Paschal Mystery. The dying and the rising is the great pattern of life and the pattern of our spiritual journey.

Let me make an application to our lives. We're very busy, doing well, learning, getting a lot accomplished. It's Palm Sunday. Everyone is pleased with us. Everything is going as planned. Then comes Holy Thursday, and while things are going as planned, we have that sense that something is beginning to change. We cannot put our finger on it but we know from the past when changes are about to happen. (My uncle had a saying that describes this: "waiting for the other shoe to fall.") Then it's Good Friday. Everything has fallen apart. We don't know what to do. Our friends come over to help us and all they can do is mouth platitudes. "It's God's will." " You are strong, I am sure you can handle it." "Why are you making such a big deal about it?" " God must be preparing you for something important." We feel like giving them nails and a hammer so they can take part in the crucifixion. Then Holy Saturday arrives and God feels so distant. There is a feeling of dryness, emptiness, feelings so different from the usual close sense of God's presence. We are sure that God has abandoned us. Then comes our Easter. There is light at the end of the tunnel. Things seem to be coming together again. We rise out of our situation and can hardly believe there's life after what we've been through. We cannot believe that we have survived this experience. And sometimes we have an Ascension Thursday experience of God that is healing and comforting—a real sense of God's abiding presence. We say to ourselves, "After all this, at last I've arrived! Now I can move into my twilight years with my God with great confidence." Then what happens? Palm Sunday starts all over again. The cycle continues . . . and continues. That's what it means to die and rise again. That's what it means to walk in the "footsteps of Christ"—it is to live the Paschal Mystery.

These cycles have various speeds. Sometimes we can experience the cycle in one morning before lunch. We rise early, all bushy-tailed and in tune, proclaiming with Isaiah, "Here I am, God, send me." Off to work we go and what a day it is. The best—this is our Palm Sunday. Then at 9:43 A.M. we see "that one"—you know who I mean—wants an appointment with us at 10:30. Oh no, what does she want? Every time we go in, there seems to be a problem. We call up one of our friends to get some advice or at least some comfort. It is Holy Thursday. Nothing bad has happened yet, but there is a feeling that trouble is coming. We go in for our 10:30 appointment: there are some difficulties that need to be taken care of and we are being blamed. We try to explain to no avail: she never listens. That person knows exactly how to push our most "sacred buttons." Her effect on us suggests a need for therapy. It is Good Friday, we feel as if we are hanging on the Cross. "Lord, why have you forsaken me!" The hour after the meeting is the "pits." There is no energy to do anything except resolve this difficulty, which was not our fault in the first place. It is Holy Saturday. We do our best and the problems get solved. The boss recognizes how quickly it was handled and says we are due for a commendation. Job well done. It is Easter. Wait a minute: what if we do our best and get nothing back from the boss? Good question; what do you think? The Paschal Mystery is a series of dying and rising on a regular basis.

As we live out the implications of relationships, our humanity, and the seasons of our lives, we are open to what's happening and sensitive to our reactions. We get insight into what our real work is on this journey. It's called being fully alive and fully human. We need a savior once we realize we are human. We all know some people who apparently think they do not need a savior. They have sublimated all their human passions and foibles so much they no longer feel. They live in temporary denial. I say "temporary" because a time will come when they'll be invited to greater freedom by the Lord. Until that happens these self-recognized perfect people are really difficult. We prefer people who have experienced the ups and downs of life and the paschal cycles. When they share with us, we are supported on our own journey. Being spiritual is not playing a role. It is being open to the activity of the Spirit on our journey, which frees us more and more to respond to the promptings of the Spirit as they apply to the events of our everyday lives.

In all that I have said it is important that the tradition of our Christian faith come alive for us: two thousand years of the Creed; two thousand years of the Sacraments; two thousand years of the Word of God; two thousand years of the Commandments as interpreted by Christ; two thousand years of devotions; two thousand years of women and men living their lives for the honor and glory of God; two thousand years of the writings of the "superstars" of our tradition; two thousand years of the music, art, invention, and scientific discoveries inspired by people's faith; and two thousand years of reaching out to serve the needs of others. We need to celebrate this faith, to be proud of it, to be nourished by it, to cherish it on a deeper level. This, in spite of other voices today making it appear that there is something wrong with being faithful to our beliefs—as if we will be underdeveloped persons if we are faithful.

There is a certain peace and confidence that comes from knowing that the message of Christ is alive and well. The faith we draw on has been tested and retested by hundreds of generations in every possible cultural and ethical climate. They have been found reliable and useful for so many people for so long under many different circumstances.

I know some of you are thinking, "Well the churches are not that perfect and holy." That is true, because the church is us—you and me. Our churches are living organisms. As we go through our seasons of the Paschal Mystery, so the church goes through her seasons. History spells this out quite clearly. A marvelous professor of Church history in the seminary used to tell us that historians never get upset with the events of the present because as they look back they can see similar situations which happened centuries before. Situations which the church survived and even helped her grow in grace. When I hear people today saying, "These are the worse of times . . . ," I know their grasp of Church history is weak. The Lord said, "I will be with you until the end of time." All the evidence of two thousand years points to the fact that He has been true to His word.

So as we go through our Palm Sundays, Holy Thursdays, Good Fridays, Holy Saturdays, Easter Sundays, and sometimes Ascension Thursdays, we shouldn't be surprised that the Church has experienced and will experience the same thing. How else will she grow and mature through the ages? How else will we grow and mature through our lifetime?

I invite you to take a second look at the Church if you have drifted away; there is more than meets the eye in the Church. Rediscover the truth, wisdom, beauty, knowledge, ritual, grace, and the holiness of people. At the same time see the healing, forgiveness, and open arms of the Savior imaged in the Church. I invite you to take another look. The Church is not perfect, so what? There is so much of value here, two thousand years of experience and know-how. What a gift! Thank you, Lord.

I will use the words of Psalm 116 as a prayer to keep with us on the spiritual journey: "I will walk in the presence of the Lord in the land of the living." My whole being I will place in the presence of the Lord. It reminds me of that song, "All of me, why not take all of me? / Can't you see I am no good without you? / You took the part which once was my heart, / So why not take all of me?"

And I will pray to live my life in union with everyone in the land of the living with the whole cosmos. Our world is wonder filled. As I am writing this, I can hear the sea in the background, the seagulls japing, the birds singing, and I can see the sun breaking through the early morning mist. I am at my favorite place on the New Jersey shore. But even here I know that our world is not a perfect one. What I see and experience sometimes breaks my heart, but that too is part of the Paschal Mystery. "I will walk in the presence of the Lord in the land of the living" (Ps 116).

How pleased I was to come across a book entitled *The Spiritual Journey—Critical Thresholds and Stages of Adult Spiritual Genesis* by Francis Nemeck and Marie Theresa Coombs. For a long time I was searching for a overview of the spiritual journey that would speak to contemporary people and show it as the true adventure that it is. Nemeck and Coombs have taken the teaching of St. John of the Cross, prayed over it, and conceptualized it in such a way that it *does* speak to contemporary people. I have taken their material, prayed over it, and created my own approach with their help. It is with great joy that I present this to you.

The journey consists of the simple and yet difficult task of allowing God to take over our lives. The contemplative journey is essentially one of surrender.

Let us look at a map of this journey. Just look upon me as a popularizer with a strong desire to give people the "rest of the story" that our tradition contains. This is just one of many approaches.

St. John of the Cross saw three paths on the journey. The first is the path of the goods of heaven. This is praying and living for the purpose of being rewarded. We are doing this in order to get to heaven. We start out on our path to heaven by working to build up our virtues, to become better persons, but we cannot end there. There is nothing wrong with that intention, but there is more to the journey than that. We begin to realize it is not a matter of reward. We pray to God, "Lord, I want to be on this journey, regardless of rewards or experiences. My hands are empty, you fill them." That's one route. The more we can say, "Here I am," the more God will fill us with the Spirit. Realize it is an arduous task to come to this point. It goes against our human nature and it takes time before we learn to say, "Here I am." We can't speed up the process; it isn't under our control. Some may say, "So what's wrong with wanting to get to heaven?" I answer "Nothing, but there is more to the journey than just that."

Here is an example to consider. I have an eighty-seven-year-old mother. She lives at home with a live-in caretaker. When I am home on Thursday, I go over and assist my mom in taking care of some of her financial matters, listen to how things are going, take her out for a ride, and do the shopping for the week. I do it because I love her and each visit has its own surprises. What would you think of me if I said to you that the reason I was doing this was that I wanted to be remembered in her will when she dies? You would say, "That's a hell of a reason for being good to your mother. Shame on you." Similarly people who are good simply—and I stress the word "simply"—for the reward of heaven are looking for the "payoff." They miss the point that they are loving and being loved by their God right now by the way they are loving others.

Another path that John of the Cross speaks of is being good for the goods of earth, to be blessed now. We have to plan and care about the things of earth, but no matter how much we care and do, they are never completely under our control. For example, we might be eagerly looking forward to having a good time on vacation; we want it to be perfect. We get so into wanting to have a good time that we do not have a good time. Our excessive striving ruins the inner freedom needed for authentic pleasure—even a good time. My niece Michele gave me a little plaque with the saying, "Are we having fun yet?" She loves saying "Are we having fun yet?" at our family gatherings, especially when we have been laughing so hard we cannot catch our breath.

When we are happy, we don't have to ask. The principle applies widely. The perfect job, the ideal house, the coolest car—if we count too heavily on them fulfilling us, they let us down. T. S. Eliot has said, "Teach us to care and not to care, teach us to sit still." In all of this the having or the not having is not a sign and measure of God's love. If we do good, looking for an increase in worldly things as a sign of God's love, we are in big trouble. There is a need for detachment from the goods of the earth. But detachment does not mean disinterest concerning the goods of earth.

The third way of John of the Cross is "the straight and narrow way." It is the way of doing all for the sake of Christ, and Him only. We do not look for the reward of heaven, we do not look for the goods of the earth, but we do it for the Lord. It is this third way which I would like to share with you in greater detail now.

We could summarize the three paths in this way.

- Yes, we yearn for the goods of heaven—but not only that.
- Yes, we yearn for the goods of the earth—but not only that.
- Yes, we yearn for God—and only that.

In John's schema, the paths cross each other at our death. For John, our personal death is the ultimate moment of contemplation because we finally surrender everything to be present to God. John was a poet, so he tried to describe the movements through the image "the dark night of the soul." We could describe the process as "the two-armed embrace of God." One arm is the seducing arm (as when Jeremiah complained that God seduced him) and the other is the chastising arm. One arm is the comforting arm and the other is the arm of purification. Death is God's final embrace—a big squeeze takes place! As our last resistance dies, we are completely embraced by God. As we finally complete our life on earth, at the last squeeze, God squeezes our false self out, and we are empty and ready to be completely filled by God. Then we are lost in the everything of God. John uses the word "*nada*"—nothing—when we are empty of the false self and John uses the word "*todo*"—all—when we are completely filled with the true self. I will be talking more about the false self and the true self in a later chapter. For now, the true self is those parts of us that are in conformity with gospel values; the false self is made up of those parts that are not in conformity with gospel values. My grandfather used to hug me with what I thought was all of his might. When I would say to him, "Grandpa you hug me too tight," he would say back to me, "It is because I love you very much."

The contemplative genius of John of the Cross's teaching is that by having nothing, we have everything. This having nothing at first is not easy to understand. What it means is that when we finally detach ourselves from things other than God—detach in the sense of not seeing them as a source of ultimate fulfillment and happiness for us—then we are ready to attach ourselves to God. In so doing, we really possess everything else because we possess our God. So that in "having nothing" we have everything because we have the source of all things.

Another way of putting it is this. We are trying to get out of the way and allow God to do what needs to be done. We surrender everything to have everything. We let go of all in order to possess all. It is like the parable of the person who found a jewel of great price in his field. What did he do? He sold all he had to buy the field. We cannot possess God, cannot control God; all we can do is consent and surrender to God, leaving our attachments to everything else behind.

Now let us look at the stages of this journey—a better word than "stages" would be "thresholds"—of growth and also limitation as human beings. As we grow we have what is called a "the crisis of limitation"—a period in our lives when we realize our finiteness and need for God. This inner need can be conscious or unconscious, but it is in all of us in all that we are and do.

Let me list the various points, stages, or thresholds for you: Inception, Individual Creation, Pre-immersion, Immersion in Creation, Emergence through Creation, Personal Conversion, Spiritual Engagement, Spiritual Marriage, and Personal Death. They sound quite profound but in reality they are stages that correspond to our human growth.

Inception

This contemplative journey of relationship with God starts with inception, not conception. The relationship starts when we were a thought in God's mind: That's how far back the relationship goes. Psalm 139 captures this stage:

When my bones were bring formed, carefully put together in my mother's womb, when I was growing there in secret, you knew that I was there—You saw me before I was born. The days allotted to me had all been recorded in your book before any of them even began (Ps 139:15–16a).

From inception, God has been in communication with us in His first language—silence. It is good to know that we are known and loved profoundly from the very beginning.

Individual Creation

Then there is the moment of conception. For nine months we are in our mother's womb, we are in silence and yet we are communicated to in many ways by our mother's movements, moods, even her eating habits and the enviroment around her. We are in that wonderful sea of liquid and God's willing embrace of love. Our inner formation is taking place already. So much is being transmitted to us.

We are born and we come into the world and begin to be formed in a new way. There is so much we need to learn. In one sense we are being formed and yet in another we are being de-formed. Being drawn more and more away from the memory of the resting. The child in us seems to be slowly dying. The spontaneous contemplative child withers. Our contemplative awareness is dimmed.

Did you ever wonder why we like being near the water? Why do you suppose we love to walk alone in silence by a river, creek, or the ocean. It's the call to remember, to return to that sacred and safe space, to cherish that special quiet time in our mother's womb, completely resting in the presence of God.

Pre-immersion

Birth is the start of a new journey—a new becoming. In the beginning, we are immersed in things and we are being cared for. Our security needs are taken care of, our control needs are taken care of, our affection needs are taken care of. I should say they are *hopefully* being taken care of. If there is anything actually missing or perceived to be missing, it becomes an issue in later life for all of us. Our actions are not based on any convictions of our own.

We are pre-emergent individuals. We are acting on the convictions of what others think is proper and right. We are still not eating, drinking, wearing, walking, talking, praying according to our own being; we are just going along with the flow up to a certain point. Eventually it becomes our journey and no one else's, but that will take time.

We are picking up a lot of information: how to behave socially, how to take care of ourselves. Listening and reading are giving us facts on which to build our life. We are being taught how to handle or not handle our emotions. We are being introduced into the concept of God and how God is part of our lives. We are receiving much and storing it up to use or not use as we grow up.

There is a favorite cartoon of mine which pictures a baby with her mother. First she goes to the newspaper. She's told "No, don't touch." Then she grabs a book. She's told, "No, don't touch." Then she grabs a glass. She's told, "No, don't touch." In the last frame, she's given a bowl of cereal. So the child says "No," to the mother and pushes the bowl away just the way she has been taught not to touch.

This is not a chronological development. It's possible that some people could be sixty or more and still be in pre-emergent life—just doing what they are told. They've never done anything on their own. To emerge means they have to leave behind a sense of security, perhaps a set of habits, a way of life: to cross a threshold that leaves them feeling unsettled. It's another birth. All births are traumatic. They go from a position of comfort, identity, and boundaries to a land of discomfort, confused identity, and ambiguous or nonexistent boundaries. They expose themselves to new forces outside their control.

Immersion in Creation

There is schooling, planning for the future, making vocational choices. There is work to be done; there are places to go, things to be achieved.

I must increase so that God can increase.

When we become involved in that immersion process of creation, we become excited and motivated, and we start working on self-improvement. We become excited with the gathering of material things. We begin to find that there are special people in our lives and we believe that they can make us very happy. We start doing a lot of good things. The more vigorous our activity, the more good things happen to us. We develop a wonderful sense of identity about who we think we should be. Without knowing it we make ourselves the center of our lives. I, I, I, I; even when I am doing for you, the I is very present.

At some time during this stage we become aware that we are searching. We become dissatisfied with the settled life we're leading. We need to move in some way.

We begin to develop a sense of wanting some space. We're not sure what to do with it, but increasingly we become aware that we need spaces in our lives.

We begin to suffer what can be called a "wound of creation": it seems the material things that we have acquired are not giving us the satisfaction for which we had hoped. We begin also to experience the "wound of relationship": people disappoint us, even those significant others in our lives who we thought would make us happy. It is not as bad as I make it seem, but it is unsettling and disappointing.

We begin to become aware of certain things very quickly. First, we discover that we have our own individuality, we don't need to run with the crowd. Second, we often discover a sense of vocation. "There has to be more to this than I'm doing." Finally, we begin to evaluate our life's trophies. "What do they mean? I have certain degrees, accomplishments, accumulations, and recognition, but what do they really mean?" How much of my life do I want to spend dusting my trophies, not to mention gathering new ones?

It isn't always clear, of course, but a dawning sense of neediness can come over us in regard to God. We begin to realize that God needs to be more part of our lives. We need to have someone journey with us who really understands us. We need to know ourselves as vulnerable and not see that as a failure or a sign of weakness. We learn on a deeper level that we can't go it alone. We know now like we have never known before that it doesn't pay to try to remain isolated and overly independent.

Emergence through Creation

The emergence through creation, as John of the Cross talks about it, begins when, in some way or another, we begin to realize we not only need God in our lives but we need to have a deeper relationship with God. We want to have values over and above those we have been following—not only have them, but also to own those values: step out and claim them.

Now we emerge from creation. Now the story line reverses. Now we must decrease so that God can increase. How do we learn that? If we are in a relationship, we intuitively understand how we have to decrease. The self-centered ego has to diminish in order that a "we" can emerge and be created. The "I" must decrease so that God can further increase in my life.

When that begins to happen and we want to become more explicitly involved with our God, then we begin to experience what is called in mystical literature the "night of the sense." We begin to experience the full extent of our selfishness, but we begin to face it without blame, shame, anger, or discouragement. This night is difficult. John of the Cross says that here storms begin to brew on the quiet sea of our life.

He calls the first of these storms *dizziness*. This dizziness is induced when our established notions of values and of how to do things or the traditional answers to life's situations are called into question and we become uncertain of what we used to know. Our minds are in turmoil and we feel our faith is shaken. Some of these shifts are subtle, others are more obvious. Perhaps it's about the Eucharist, perhaps about closest friends or marriage partner—where do I stand and what do I believe? Did I bargain for this? Do I really want this, or him or her? The usual sharp lines, clear answers, and comfortable procedures are all out of focus.

Of course, sooner or later, we question our faith in God and our respect for the sacred. John calls this the storm of *blasphemy*. We realize that all is not well between God and self. We often feel resentment, or dryness, or distance or all of these. We question God's love for us. After all, what's in this for us? What is the nature of the reward for all our efforts? We don't plan or schedule this, we just find ourselves moved along these lines.

We don't want to be alone during this storm. This is where some kind of communal support is necessary. Maybe it's one person who knows about this; maybe it is a community of people who can support our faith. As we get dizzier and angrier, we may need to hold on to the faith of others for awhile.

After the storm of blasphemy could come what John of the Cross calls the storm of *fornication*. We develop a powerful neediness, wanting to be connected, embraced, valued, to be a part of something or someone to affirm us. Our old emotional strength and independence fails us. We used to say it didn't matter if we were thanked or not. Now it becomes crucial. Now we're easily hurt. We feel like the elder son in Luke's Gospel story of the prodigal son. He has been faithful and confronts the father. We ask, "When do you kill the fatted calf for me?" We accuse God of taking care of the weak, while we who have been faithful and strong for so long are ignored. When is it our turn to be surprised by extravagance?

We all have some periods of this. Not all three storms, perhaps, but they come in some form or other. We absorb these shocks and finally say, "I walk in the presence of the Lord. I walk with my dizziness, my precarious faith, my desire to belong, all my inner distortions." We look in the mirror and see this person who is far from perfect, walking in the presence of the Lord. Earlier we were trying for a perfect life—neat, clean, orderly. Now we accept more of ourselves, the garbage of our lives, and we realize that this bedraggled self is the one that God loves. (By the way, garbage is nothing more than a sign that there is life in the house: if there was no one living at home there would be no garbage.) It is the false self that has failed, died, and sinned who walks in the presence of God's loving gaze. We walk right into the middle of our "stuff." We walk into the valley of darkness, walk through it, not around it. What we have experienced we have endured, because we love God and want to walk the journey of growth in spirituality.

We have to understand that while we are falling apart, we are still being cared for. This dissolution creates energy, strengthens our faith, and tests our love. If we don't understand or believe this, then it makes perfect sense to run away. We run backward to a more secure time, like a child returning home, never to mature. Sometimes when this is suppressed, we see it come out in bizarre ways. We have been so sweet and shiny for fifty years, and now we get mean, our language becomes foul, and we are an unholy terror! Where did that come from? (Suppression might be one place.) Either we make peace with it now or it will come back to haunt us later on!

At an earlier stage of development if storms like these came up, we'd make a resolution to solve the problem. At a more mature stage, we just wait it out: This, too, shall pass. We don't run—we run the rapids! We find a spiritual companion who understands the process and who will encourage us not to reach for resolution band-aids.

It is at this stage that contemplative prayer begins to flourish in our lives. Partially out of fatigue, we stop trying to figure things out and we surrender. Every answer is inadequate, every technique is flawed. God becomes more mysterious at every turn. Everything we suppress becomes more active—anger, sensuality, fear. They all have control over us, at least at times. Finally, we surrender. You win, God. And God graciously responds, "No, you finally win."

The fruit of this experience of the "night of the sense" is a letting go of our attachment to things, persons, and programs for happiness. The "night" shakes us at the root of our being and begins a process of re-creation. While all this is going on, our relationship with God is nourished and sustained by pure faith.

The Sacrament that has sustained us in this journey has been the Eucharist. There are a number of reasons for saying this. When we start experiencing falling apart, we are searching for a deeper union with our God. The Eucharist is a symbol of that deeper union. It reminds us over and over again that we are loved and that we are not alone.

The late Joseph Campbell, who has written extensively on mythology, was once a Catholic. He tells the story of a type of Eucharist in ancient Mexico and Central America, where people used to have a soccer match between two teams. The stadium would be packed for this event, which was also a religious ceremony. When the game was over the winning team would go up to the king to be crowned for the victory, then the captain of the winning team would be slain. His heart was taken out and eaten by everyone who participated in the game, for they wanted to share in his strength and goodness. Is that not what Eucharist is about? The winning captain of the team, Jesus, sacrificed Himself so that we might share in His strength and ability over and over again.

When we're going through the "storms" mentioned by John of the Cross, we need to know that the one we love loves us enough to give His body and blood for us. Otherwise it may not be worth our dying to our false self.

Personal Conversion

If we can say yes to all the storms of dizziness, blasphemy, and fornication, that is when conversion takes place. We've had earlier conversions that we call "Christian or religious conversions"; now we have the "personal conversion," the ultimate surrendering to God. When we can endure the storms John describes and still remain faithful, then our conversion is real. We are committed. We are ready for the demands of a *serious* relationship. We are like the disciples after Jesus calmed the storm. We've let go of the fantasies of our youth, when we were so virtuous in our eyes and the eyes of others. Now we believe on a much deeper level because we have gone through that period of doubting and questioning. Now we really trust because we have experienced the dizziness and confusion of trying to do it all ourselves. Now we really love on a deeper level because we have been looking for love in all the wrong places and have tasted the eventual bitterness of this search. We're getting real and getting related. John uses the term "night of the spirit" to describe this stage.

As John puts it, the light of the night of faith begins to be transformed within us. The longing, the desire of hope continues to burn within us, but the living flame of love begins to burn more brightly. This living flame of love is taking all that energy that was driving us crazy, making us dizzy and lustful, and transforming it. But not by us. We are not doing the transforming. If it weren't for the prior confusion, we wouldn't have a mature faith. It is the energy released in our battle to be connected in love that is now transformed into fidelity in love. For it is our inner spirit that is being purified. Now we are involved with the God of both arms that I described above.

The biblical image of God as the potter becomes real. We feel shaped; we feel like we've been put through a reconstruction process. We surrender to a power we can't control but we trust. In one sense we give up on ourselves and let God form us, so we feel inert like clay. We say to God, "I quit. You choose the shape." Perhaps we should call it a *spirituality of fatigue*. God wears us out. It is like a coach who has been trying to tell a player how to hit the ball and she keeps wanting to do her own way. Finally the coach says to herself, "I will say no more, I will let her do it her way and see where it gets her." After a period of no success the player finally is ready to hear what the coach has to say.

When conversion takes place, when we really want a deeper intimacy with God, we rediscover the value and power of the sacrament of reconciliation. This is the sacrament of ongoing conversion. There is a conscious desire to stay the course and we see the value of the frequent celebration of the Sacrament.

The fruits of the night of the spirit are manifested in different ways. It could be the realization that we have been overidentifying with our roles in life—our job has been a sign of our worth—the letting go of a particular addiction or emotion. Our image of God is changing in a way that makes for a more intimate relationship: a deepening of our trust and ability to surrender to God in areas of our lives where in the past we did not want divine interference. It is an embrace of the joy of experiencing the overwhelming mercy of God toward us.

Does this mean that these storms are over—the dizziness, blasphemy, and fornication? No, they will still be experienced, but they come in a different way, with God working more and more on us at deeper levels of our being. The difference is, we know what is happening, and God's healing power can do its work quicker because of our cooperation.

Spiritual Engagement and Marriage

If we allow the messy part to flourish, if we can wait out the storms of passions of every color, if we can maintain an inner silence while our passions are noisy and threatening, these energies can make us more attentive to what we truly believe, whom we truly love, what we truly desire. This isn't an idea or a mental construct, it pervades our whole being.

We live in hope. We don't know where these storms will throw us. We take a real risk in facing our seamy side and showing and offering it to God. But this is what is required to be faithful to the journey. We have been promised that we are not going to be alone. Our love will have a vitality and richness that we would be missing if we didn't live through the struggle. We are living a life of love, not just service.

We are experiencing the wound of consuming love. It is like the refiner's fire. The death of our false self is experienced on a deeper level. There is a greater compassion for the world and the cosmos and there is an intuitive knowledge of the restructuring of our being. It is a real living-out of that phrase: "I must decrease: God must increase."

Personal Death

The final threshold is death. For some who have made the journey there is a quick consummation at the time of death. As a priest I've seen many people die. Some of them may have had struggles all their lives, but at the time of death, the struggle quiets and I see a deep peace come over them. They die with smiles on their faces that are just beautiful. It isn't that they've resigned themselves to dying. It just that they've accomplished what they've been trying so hard to have happen: they've been united fully with their God. In their final stages, they have become nothing, so that when the final squeeze of God comes, then they have everything.

John of the Cross says at this point we have "*nada, nada, nada*" (nothing, nothing, nothing) and then after the moment of death, "*todo, todo, todo*": we have everything.

Please remember it is the Lord who is leading us through these stages of the journey. With each stage or threshold of growth, we experience our limitations and the expansiveness of God. As we grow we realize our finiteness and our need for God. This inner need can be conscious or unconscious, but it is there in all of us. Our God is the initiator leading us through thresholds of Inception (where we are aware that we have always been a thought in the mind of God), Individual Creation (where the thought becomes flesh at our conception), Pre-immersion (where we are formed by the values and attitudes of those around us), Immersion in Creation (where our initial journey is one of increasing ourselves and decreasing God), Emergence through Creation (where we are faced with serious issues in our lives that cause us to decrease ourselves and grow to increase the influence of God in our lives), Personal Conversion (where a deeper personal conversion takes place which is no longer just religious), Spiritual Engagement (where the storms of blasphemy, dizziness, and fornication are transformed to faith, hope, and charity), Spiritual Marriage (where the relationship with God becomes a yearning for consuming love), and Personal Death (where the moment of transformation is complete). These sound quite profound, but this journey never ends: it is not just a straight line to our destiny, but the spiral staircase that Thomas Keating talks about as deepening the intimacy with every turn of the stair.

4 ❋

Thomas Merton as a Paradigm of the Spiritual Journey

I would like to share with you some thoughts about my spiritual relationship with Thomas Merton. It started in my high school days in the '40s with the reading of his classic *The Seven Storey Mountain*. The book impressed me so much that I wanted to visit the monastery in Kentucky where he lived. I was joined in my enthusiasm by my classmate Tony Padovano. To our surprise, our parents gave us permission to make a retreat at Gethsemani, Merton's monastery. We got a Greyhound bus from the Newark, New Jersey, depot and heading down to Louisville, Kentucky. When we arrived we stayed at the YMCA for the evening, and the next day caught the train for Gethsemani. Although we were the youngest men on that retreat, we lived the retreat schedule to the fullest. We joined the monks at all their hours of prayer and enjoyed the good food served to the retreatants, especially the cheese and bread. We saw Merton briefly and only from a distance. We were filled with great joy that we could be in this holy and sacred space. There are plenty of funny stories I tell about our monastic adventure—how our luggage was delayed for two days, how we had to endure the looks we got from some of the retreatants because of our clothes and appetites. We could not resist the cheese and bread: we had the usual growing appetites of teenagers. At our table was a very serious retreatant who was fasting—I still remember the looks that we got from him as we ate away. The monk who woke us up for the morning vigil loved slamming the door of our room against the bottom portion of our metal beds. The suddenness of the "wake-up call" and the cold of the morning had me standing in front of the mirror over the sink brushing my teeth without moving my toothbrush. Every time I have visited Gethsemani since then, that rush of memories fills me. That was the beginning of my relationship with Merton that has spanned a half-century of my spiritual journey.

I believe that the life of Thomas Merton can serve as a working model for the spiritual journey for others as well as myself. By "working model" I do not mean the details of his life, but the movements that took place in his life. The stages or thresholds that he experienced are in many ways not unlike what we all go through in our own way. Nobody's saying that Merton was perfect. He wasn't. That's one of the reasons he is so attractive to contemporary people. He was on a journey. He was alive. He was deeply human. He was profoundly spiritual.

At this point I would like to bring in my friend Basil Pennington. I met Basil first at St. Joseph's Monastery in Spencer, Massachusetts, in 1969. We co-authored a book on priesthood, *Living Our Priesthood Today,* in 1987. We are crossroad friends: not in frequent contact with one another, and yet whenever our paths cross, the meetings have been enriching. Usually he has gone before or is coming after me as we both travel around the United States and beyond, giving workshops and retreats on Centering Prayer or *lectio divina.* He has written an excellent book entitled, *Thomas Merton, Brother Monk* and my comments on Merton will be based on my reading of Basil Pennington's work on him. This chapter results from my belief that Merton is a very important person for you to know, and from my hope that he will speak to you in a very special way as he has to me.

In talking of the life of Merton, Basil observes:

> Father Louis's [Merton's religious name] life is rather interesting and neatly divided into distinct parts of equal length. Twenty

seven years outside the monastery, twenty seven years inside the monastery. The two halves parallel each other in interesting ways. Both parts profited from a strong discipline administered by a loving disciplinarian in the beginning—actually, about seven years. Both encouraged him in his writing and put him through paces he did not wholly enjoy but bore good fruit.

In the first seven of the first twenty-seven years the "loving disciplinarian" was his mother. In the second half it was his first abbot, Dom Frederick Dunne, who just took a tremendous liking to him. His mother insisted on his doing things correctly, and the abbot kept on saying, "Write, write, write." In his early years in the monastery life we hear Merton saying, "I don't want to write. I've come here to be alone." He had entered religious life with a preconceived idea of what he would do. Pennington continues on Merton's life:

> After their passing (both mother and abbot died rather young in his journey), he was much more on his own, especially with regard to his writing. After each of their deaths, there was no one in his life who really understood him, no one to walk consistently with him. He could not fully trust any one. He did some wild and stupid things.

> So the pattern was seven years of discipline, then a period of freedom during which he had to learn to listen to the Spirit. In each case toward the end of the period he developed a friendship with a special woman, there was times of particular enlightenment and finally a breakthrough to another life.

In his first twenty-seven years, the special woman was Baroness Catherine de Hueck who introduced him to working at Friendship House in Harlem and to social action. The period of enlightenment in that first period would be when, somehow or other, he became well aware of the presence of God in things. The final breakthrough to another life in the first period was his entrance into the Trappists.

The second portion of his life, more like the life of the spirit, was more subtle. The special woman in his life was the nurse he fell in love with in Louisville in 1966. The relationship lasted only a few months. This experience affirmed for him that he was lovable as himself. She didn't know him as an author, she didn't know him as a famous person, she just knew him as a man. In this celibate yet romantic relationship, this part of his life was affirmed. He was found lovable for himself alone.

As that particular moment of enlightenment was taking place, he began giving up his preconceived ideas. He had a profound experience in Sri Lanka at a Buddhist shrine where everything made sense and nothing made sense. It was here that he got in touch with the transcendent reality of God. Notice that he didn't give up his faith: he would never give up his Christian faith for Buddhism. But he did experience a crossing over, a new insight that made him realize how transcendent God was in his life. Then finally, there came his untimely death which for Merton was the ultimate act of contemplation—resting in the presence of God.

That is Basil's loving overview of the two twenty-seven-year halves of Merton's life (1915–68). The Trappists, at this time, have no intention to petition for sainthood for Merton. They are convinced that this man is a marvelous human being, a loving figure leading people who want to fall in love with God. Today, thirty years after his death, his writings and recorded talks still have a powerful effect on people.

Let's look at Merton's journey in light of the stages and thresholds I discussed in the previous chapter.

Inception

Thomas Merton was in the mind of God from the beginning. There was a loving relationship and an awareness on God's part of who he was going to be. When the time came for his conception, this thought in God's mind was about to be enfleshed. It is essential in our journeys never to forget the bond that exists between us and our God right from the beginning.

Individual Creation

At the moment of our conception God brings into being a human made in His image and likeness. We are already spiritual beings. Now we are human beings who are "becoming." During that time in the womb we are aware of the different energies around our conception. Are we wanted? Was our mother feeling well? How was the atmosphere in the family? Did Mom take care of herself? All this information is coming our way. In the meantime, God is communicating with us in His language of silence. In regard to Merton, it seems that he was wanted and his birth was anticipated with great joy.

Pre-immersion

This period refers to the early years, especially the first six or seven years. During these years, we are being formed unconsciously. We are picking up a lot of information concerning our social behavior, the care of ourselves physically, the use of our intellect, our dealing with our emotions. The seeds are being planted in regard to our relationship with our God. We are receiving all this information; we do not quite own it, but it is part of us because others have told us it is important. So much of the foundation upon which our life is to be built is formed at this time.

Merton was born in France on January 31, 1915. The following year he moved to the United States with his parents. His father and mother were what we might call "bohemians." They were very interested in the arts and very much "with it." His mother was from a well-to-do family which was fond of art, writing, and the finer things in life. Thomas had a relationship with his grandparents on his mother's side. They were dear to him and left quite an impact. For example, his grandfather was bigoted against Catholics. It was hard for Merton to break through to become a Catholic for many years because he had heard a lot of negative stories about Catholics as a young boy. His mother died of cancer when he was seven: This loss of nurturing had a deep impact on him. As a child, he saw her sick and suffering. His father then became more influential in his life.

Immersion in Creation

There comes a time in our lives when we begin to start to take ownership of the things of our lives. It is gradual. It has to do with our self worth, our acceptance of our talents, our willingness to be more open to the experiences of life; the knowledge that we are called to be responsible for our actions. In a sense we feel like "the king of the mountain." This is all lived out in school, travel, friends, the experiences of life, and the role models that we choose. We have a desire to be loved and people around us are important in our development. We plunge into the work of the world. Perhaps it could be put this way: "I must increase so that God can increase." It is a period of life when more is better. Some have put it this way: My stuff must increase; God's must decrease.

Back to Merton. In 1926 he was studying in France. He found this to be a traumatic experience. He felt that he was in a prison. His health began to deteriorate and he developed signs of tuberculosis. In 1930 his grandfather left him an endowment, so that at the age of fifteen he was financially independent. His father died when Merton was sixteen. Here again he experienced trauma as he watched his father waste away from a brain tumor. So by the time he was sixteen, he had watched both of his parents die. He then came under the influence of his godfather, Tom Bennett. Bennett was a delightful man of the world who just loved to be an insider. He was the one who encouraged young Tom Merton to have a cigarette, a few drinks, and a good time. After all, life is for living. Tom loved his godfather, of course. He was now living in England with Tom Bennett as his role model, but Merton was really on his own, going from boarding school to boarding school, family to family.

Everything was going well. He was having a wonderful time, but he got himself in trouble just as he was starting classes in Cambridge. He got a young woman pregnant and she had his child. His godfather, Tom Bennet took care of her and the child. Eventually the mother moved to London. Merton always wondered throughout his life whether he had done the right thing, whether he should have stayed in the woman's life or let his godfather take care of her.

She and the child died during the blitz in the early 1940s. He knew there was something missing in him that would allow such behavior. He regretted it all his life. He writes in *The Seven Storey Mountain*,

> It did not take much reflection on the year at Cambridge to show me that all my dreams of fantastic pleasures and delights were crazy and absurd. Everything I had reached out for had turned to ashes in my hands. And I myself, into the bargain, had turned out to be an extremely unpleasant sort of person: vain, self-centered, dissolute, weak, undisciplined, sensual, obscene and proud. In other words, I was a mess. Even my own face in the mirror was enough to disgust me.

His godfather, his last family link, disowned him. He had encouraged the wild side of Tom and then disowned him when he went too far. I guess the godfather's action falls into the commandment: "Do your own thing but don't get caught." So rejection, loss, and failure were part of his early life.

By the time he was twenty he had crossed the Atlantic nine times. This wasn't by transatlantic flight, but by ship during World War I and the Roaring '20s. All the ordinary supports were gone and you can see how someone like this was being pushed to get his life together. It is amazing when we look at the first part of great people's lives. They often have terrible loses early. Many artists and musicians work out of the energy of early pain, loss, and separation. They were pushed to mature faster and got more than what they bargained for.

In 1934 he came to the United States and began to settle down. (He didn't become a citizen until after he entered the monastery.) When people have had a difficult and confusing time, they often tend to rely on a value system other than their own. In his case, he joined the Communist Party at Columbia University for a while. It was the thing to do. Why did he do that? He says, "Because this was a way I could repent for the wrong I had done, to try to undo some of the harm that I see in the world."

During this period of the spiritual journey the links that hold a person together are service and concern for others. A spiritual awareness begins to surface in one's life:

> Looking back on my episode of being in the Communist Party, I see that my inspiration to do something for the good of humankind

had been pretty feeble and abstract from the start. I was interested in doing good for only one person in the world—myself.

Merton knew his great interest in helping others was his need to wash away his own sins. Some people in social action are yelling and screaming as though the wrong was outside themselves. The outer wrongs can be healed only when one takes care of his inner disorders. The real wrongs are often inside ourselves.

His school, social life, and work in New York were all fast-paced. He was having a wonderful time even though he wasn't enjoying all of it as much as before. On the surface, Merton's life was wonderfully exciting. He was at the center of intellectual ferment which everyone at Columbia University was experiencing (this was in 1935). Nevertheless, Merton was so immersed in activity that he had no time to think about the important things in life. He seemed to be in fine condition, enjoying success; he had a full load of courses; he was involved with the *Literary Journal of Columbia* and the yearbook; he had a job at Rockefeller Center; and his cross-country running left little time for reflection.

These activities did not interfere with his social life. He put it this way. He devoted

> pulsating late nights and early mornings in dark, deafening night clubs to smoking, drinking and jazz. One got caught up in a strange animal travesty of mysticism, bound to a sea of bodies, with the rhythms jumping and throbbing in the marrow of one's bones.

But then, the night would end. He writes:

> The thing that depresses me most of all was the shame and despair that invaded my whole nature when the sun came up. All the laborers were going to work. The men, healthy and quiet, their eyes clear, had some rational purpose before them. This humiliation and sense of my own misery and of the fruitlessness of what I had done was the nearest I could get to contrition. It was a reaction of nature. It proved nothing except that I was at least morally alive, or rather that I had some faint capacity for moral life in me.

So he began to see that there was a need for a new direction in his life but he was not sure what that meant. Two things happened in 1936. His grandfather died. That was an awful blow to

him, because there went another male model in his life. The other
was that he collapsed on a Long Island train coming back from a
party. The doctors said he had spinning vertigo; that he had a
possible nervous breakdown and the beginnings of a stomach
ulcer. He wondered:

> If my nature had been more stubborn in clinging to the pleasures
> that disgusted me, if I had refused to admit that I was beaten by
> this futile search for satisfaction where it could not be found and
> if my moral and nervous constitution had not caved in under the
> weight of my own emptiness, who can tell what would have even-
> tually happened to me?

This is the language of thresholds, times in life when we are
moved, albeit unwillingly, into another area. An early threshold for
him was the pregnancy of the woman in England. Now his second
threshold was his physical collapse. He said a little earlier, "Such
was the death of the hero, the great man I wanted to be." He wanted to be like his godfather—debonair, alive, money, women,
booze, a successful writer. It sounds familiar—a lot of people want
to be like that. But the fear and the strain that something's not
working right inside turns the light on in a different way. He knew
he had to move in a new direction or things would get worse.

Emergence through Creation

In this period there is an awareness of the full extent of selfishness in one's life. It is looked at without blame, shame, anger,
or discouragement. It is looked at in the context of the whole picture. An interesting phenomenon begins to take place: a questioning of what one used to believe and hold without question,
an uncertainty about what direction to go in life. At the same
time, when a decision or direction needs to be made, one finds
that he or she is are unable to make a decision. One realizes that
the things one thought would make him or her happy are not.
One wonders: Who do I really love? Who really loves me? Who
do I belong to? These questions are immense favors from God
because they open one to a realization that perhaps there is some
truth to the saying, "I must decrease so that Christ can increase."

Merton was a bright student, he majored in English and was studying for his doctorate. He loved to read and in this period began to discover certain works that were important to him. He discovered Etienne Gilson's *Spirit of Medieval Philosophy*. As he began to read what Gilson had to say, he realized he could identify with the response to the God he was learning. He still could not identify with the usual God he heard people talking about.

> The truth is that the concept of God which I had always entertained and which I had accused Christians of teaching to the world was the concept of a being which was simply impossible. He was infinite yet finite, perfect yet imperfect, eternal and yet changing, subject to all the varieties of emotions: love, sorrow, hate, revenge that men were prey to. How could this emotional thing be without beginning or end and the creator of all. . . . If this much was a great thing, it was about all I could do at the moment. I could recognize that those who had thought about God had a good way of considering him and that those who believed in him really believed in someone. Their faith was more than a dream. Further than that, I could not go. But I was beginning to see the value of a God.

After reading Gilson, he decided to go to church. He hadn't gone to church in a long time, so when he was out on Long Island, he popped into the Episcopal Church to make a visit.

He took a course in Shakespeare with his soon-to-be friend, Mark Van Doren, and for the first time in his life he heard someone say something worthwhile about life, death, love, time, sorrow, fear, wisdom, suffering, and eternity. He read Aldous Huxley's book, *Ends and Means,* and he realized there could be a place in a person's life for prayer, for faith, for detachment, for love.

In 1938 he began to read the poetry of William Blake, which helped him to understand that one doesn't have to push away the natural energies; they are all part of the journey. Previously he had assumed that in order to be good he would have to kill all the passion, love, and vitality he felt inside himself.

Also in 1938, he met the Hindu monk Bramachari, whom he loved. He says he was influenced by the simplicity and detachment of the man who personified in the flesh so much of what Merton had been encountering in books. So Merton was prepared for this encounter by his serious reading, then he met the real thing. Because Bramachari was sensitive to Merton's Christian roots, he recommended that Merton read *The Imitation of Christ* and *The Confessions* of St. Augustine.

Merton had a history of meeting people who would lead him in the direction that was needed at that time. In September of 1938, he concluded that, "I was to become conscious of the fact that the only way to live was to live in a world that was charged with the presence and reality of God."

He saw the need for a greater awareness of the presence of God in his life. That led him for the first time to go to Sunday mass in a Catholic Church. He had passed up his usual weekend visit with his girlfriend on Long Island. He made his way to Corpus Christi Church, near Columbia University. He stayed only for the sermon. The sermon was a straightforward exposition of the Incarnation, tinged with scholastic terminology. It was what he most needed to hear that day. He had walked in on a teacher who spoke his language. He was so overjoyed at what happened that he wrote:

> When I walked leisurely down Broadway in the sun and my eyes looked about me at a new world, I could not understand what it was that had happened to make me so happy. Why was I so much at peace, so content with life? All I knew was that I walked in a new world. Even the ugly buildings of Columbia University were transfigured in it and everywhere was peace in these streets, designed for violence and noise.

Having had this marvelous experience at Mass, he did not go back. That's Merton! He didn't feel drawn to do anything about it at that time. But he did begin to read Gerald Manley Hopkins, the English Jesuit poet. Hopkins tells about his time at Oxford and his struggle about becoming a Catholic. Merton wrote in his journal, "What are you waiting for? Why are you sitting here? Why do you hesitate? You know what you ought to do, why don't you do it?"

With that in mind he decided to go to a men's mission at a local church in October 1938. He sat through the instructions and was baptized on November 16, 1938. You might think that this was his conversion. But it was just the Baptism. After that he began to wonder about what he wanted to do in his life. He said later on, "My mind was convinced, but the rest of my body was not. The conversion was a conversion of my head, not the rest of my being." Later on, talking with his friend, Bob Lax, he heard Lax say, "You know, if you're a Catholic, you should become a saint." This confused Merton. He didn't see himself as a saint. But it did make him consider that there was more that he needed to do.

Then an extraordinary thing happened to him when school began in the fall of '39. He had been up all night with his friends as usual. After a few hours sleep, they brought in some breakfast, talked, and listened to jazz. "Somewhere, in the midst of all of this," he writes, "a startling idea came to me. I am going to be a priest."

That evening he was alone again. After dinner he decided to visit the Jesuit church of St. Francis Xavier. No one was in church but he heard music coming from downstairs. They were having a Benediction service so he went down. He knew his whole life was at a crisis point. Here he was, of all people, thinking of becoming a priest.

> As the hymn was ending, the priest raised the monstrance. I looked straight at the host and I knew now who it was that I was looking at. And I said, "Yes, I want to be a priest. With all my heart I want to. If it is your will, make me a priest. Make me a priest."

The power of those last four words, "make me a priest" did not escape him. He knew the new course; his life was set for him. So by the end of 1939 he not only knew he had to have a relationship with God but he also knew this relationship had to take a new direction. Somehow he had to die to his old way of living.

He went to his friend and favorite teacher, Dan Walsh, who himself later became a priest and Trappist. Dan said, "Why don't you try the Franciscans?" So he visited the monastery on 31st Street in New York. He talked to a priest about what was going on in his life and his desire to be a priest. He said they would let him know. He decided to do the Ignatian Spiritual Exercises on his own and spent an hour each day going through the Exercises. Merton always liked to do things his way. The Ignatian Spiritual

Exercises are a series of meditations leading one into a discernment process to help hear the word of God in one's life.

Later, during a visit to Cuba, he had a tremendous experience at mass:

> When the children all cried out, "I believe in God" at the conse-
> cration . . . as sudden as the shout, and as definite, and a thousand
> times more bright there formed in my mind an awareness and an
> understanding of what had been taking place at the altar at the
> consecration. A realization of God made present by the words of
> consecration in a way that made him belong to me."

During this period the sacrament of the Eucharist becomes
a powerful means of grace. The Eucharist started to speak more
and more to him. He came back to New York in June 1940 and
returned to the Franciscans who said, "Yes, we will have you."
Merton was very happy that the direction in his life was becoming clearer. He went off to Long Island for another party. (Life
goes on!)

One night while on Long Island, he was sitting reading the
Book of Job. He heard these words inside him. "If he examines
me on a sudden, who shall answer him." He began to wonder if
being a priest is what God wanted of him. He was aware he did
not tell the Franciscans about having fathered a child and that the
mother and child were still alive.

The peace he had experienced for six months disappeared. He
felt moved to go and tell the Franciscans all the details of his life
He immediately returned to New York City, went to the monastery,
sat down with Father Edmond, whom he liked very much and
who advised him to go to confession and then tell his story. The
Franciscans said, "We cannot accept you. If we had known all the
details beforehand we would never have said yes."

So, what did he do? He decided, "Maybe I'm not meant to
live in the monastery. I will live in the world in a monastic way."
So he joined the Third Order. He began to pray the office and
went off to teach at a Franciscan college, St. Bonaventure. Most
of us, if we were rejected by Franciscans would reject a Franciscan college. Merton didn't leave any unfinished business. He
went to their school, taught there, and had a most fruitful year.

After he had taught English for a semester at St. Bonaventure in 1941, World War II began and young men were being drafted into the service. Look at his situation: He had been a member of the Communist Party. He had taken a pledge that he would never fight in a war. Now, as a Catholic, he accepted the "just war" theory. He was willing to be drafted as long as he wasn't placed in a situation of combat. These were the objections he was going to bring to the draft board. He was ready. He went determined to take a stand. But he never had a chance to say anything. He failed the physical because he had bad teeth! I am sure you know as well as I do that God has a sense of humor.

Later Dan Walsh asked him, "Why don't you go make a retreat down at the Trappist monastery in Gethsemani, Kentucky?" He made a Holy Week retreat and at the end he made the Stations of the Cross, asking, "God, if it is your will, I wish to be a Trappist." He went back to New York, and during summer school at St. Bonaventure he met Baroness Catherine de Hueck, a woman dedicated to the spiritual journey and the needs of the poor. He decided to go to Friendship House in Harlem and work with the poor. He felt he was being drawn to this. He started, but an unusual thing happened. Mark Van Doren said, "I thought you were going to be a priest? What are you doing at Friendship House?" Something clicked and Merton agreed. "That's right. That is what I had said."

So the day after Thanksgiving, he wrote and was accepted by the Trappists and was in the monastery on December 10, 1941. When it's right, everything falls into line—sometimes.

Notice what happened during this phase of the spiritual journey. He had to reassess his way of thinking. He had to let go of preconceived ideas about his life. He had doubts about his vocation, about what God wanted him to do. His social life and relationships left him empty and he knew there had to be something more to life. He had good friends around him who supported him in this quest. The Holy Spirit kept shining the light on what he had to look at in his life. It was not easy. His emotional and physical health were affected. He found himself drawn to the Church not only in his readings (the intellectual pursuit), but also emotionally and experientially in the moments of greater awareness that he experienced in the Eucharist. (As an aside, I know non-Catholics who experience the gift of tears whenever they attend Eucharist in the Roman Catholic Church. They say there is something that touches them on such a deep level they cannot control the joy they feel.)

So Merton was looking for happiness in a new place and was aware of the gift of faith that was now his as he desired to deepen his relationship with God. You would think he had arrived. No. A new journey was just beginning.

Personal Conversion and Spiritual Engagement

Going to Gethsemani was another threshold experience, involving questions of what one believes in, the uncertainty about what one is being called to do within a vocation, and the desire to belong and to be loved for one's self rather than for what one does. These are all the "night of the sense" that John of the Cross gives the names blasphemy, dizziness, and fornication. They had been faced by Merton before he entered the monastery, but now they were faced on a deeper level as the Lord moved him into greater faith, deeper trust, and genuine charity and love.

Imagine this New Yorker at twenty-seven coming to the hills of Kentucky in 1941! It was the time of his ongoing personal conversion. But, it didn't happen all at once.

He went into the monastery to make expiation for his sinful life and to atone for not being able to change things in the world. He had a great sense of freedom. He said, "I felt like a wanderer who finally came home."

Of course, the beginning is always a honeymoon period. It didn't last long. By early 1942 he was screaming within himself, "Where is the solitude?" He came for solitude and felt he had no privacy. Then, thank God, he got sick and was forced to go to the infirmary. He loved this. He writes: "I will have some solitude. I will have plenty of time to pray and to do everything I want to do without having to run all over the place answering bells." Concerning this desire for solitude and to get away from the routine he writes later that he, "did not know how to recognize as selfish these desires because they appeared as spiritual in their new disguises."

He tells how he jumped into bed in the infirmary and opened his Bible to The Canticle of Canticles, devoured three chapters, closed his eyes from time to time, waiting with expectation for lights, voices, harmonies, music of angelic choirs. In fact he got nothing. He had gone into the monastery to leave the world behind and nothing was happening. He went into the monastery for the solitude that he yearned for and had to get sick in order to get it. And when he got the solitude, it did not turn out the way he expected. Does that sound familiar?

The other thing he wished to leave behind was the burden of writing. "I don't want to write any more. I want to be a monk, living in solitude." Wonderful. "The writer in me is supposed to be dead." What happened? His own superiors were on the side of the writer. They didn't try to get rid of the writer; they encouraged him to do more writing. The next time he got sick, they had him translate a French text on the history of Cistercian life. He was learning the hard way to die to himself and his desires. That is a wonderful lesson for each one of us. God works in the context of gifts we may not want to use.

He didn't have the time nor the desire to do much journaling. But by 1947, when he took his solemn vows, he felt that he could begin to accept the fact that he would not be rid of the rules or the burden of writing. He still complained, though:

> Trappists believe that everything that costs them is God's will. Anything that makes you suffer must be God's will. If we want something, we can easily persuade ourselves it is God's will, just as long as it turns out to be difficult. What is easy is our own will, what is hard is God's. As a result, we think we have done great things because we are worn out. If we had rushed into the fields or woods and have done a great deal of damage, we are satisfied.

About his writing he says: "Just because a cross is a cross does it follow that it is the cross God intends for you?"

So he had just made solemn profession and instead of bliss and consolation, he was lamenting his fate. He didn't really accept that it is God's will that he should be a writer. No matter how hard he tried to run away from his gift, it continued to track him down. Then came a mixed blessing—an absolute surprise to him and everyone else. When his book, *The Seven Storey Mountain* was published in 1948, critics and the general public began raving about this monk's marvelous story. He realized he wasn't ever going to get away from being a writer.

(As an aside to show how times have changed, I have been told that *The New York Times* did not list it on the best-seller list because it had a religious theme. It outsold all the other best-sellers at that time. Today if you look at the list, it is amazing of how many spiritually oriented books are on the list. How times have changed.)

Merton had another surprise when he took a trip to Louisville in August of 1948. There, he looked at the world and began to realize that what he had written about the world being evil and wicked was a mistake:

> When I went through the city, I realized for the first time in my life how good the people in the world are and how much value they have in the sight of God.

So he had a best seller, saying the world is evil, and then he changed his mind! He realized that it was naive to say the world is evil. Already growth was taking place in his overall view of life.

He spent a lot of time preparing for deaconate ordination. He was beginning to feel tired and stale, he was ashamed of the fame he was receiving, and he felt terribly burdened with fan mail. He felt a responsibility to address all of it. In fact his collection of correspondence reveals his great depth and expanse of interest.

After he received deaconate he had an experience of the closeness of God, which led him to be indifferent regarding whether he was a monk or an author. He simply let it go. When he was ordained a priest in May 1949, it was a highlight in his life. His tremendous sense of the closeness of God lasted until September. He did have one embarrassing moment when in full liturgical apparel he passed out and they had to take him to the infirmary.

From September of 1949 to the end of 1950, he went through a very difficult time. He describes it like this:

> There is a conversion of the deep will to God that cannot be effected in words, barely in a gesture or ceremony. . . . "My heart is troubled within me, fear of death has fallen upon me. Fear and trembling have come upon me and darkness has covered me."

As he chanted these words from the Psalms at the divine office, he felt he was chanting about himself. It described his own experience—darkness and aloneness. He described himself during this time as lonely, small, and humiliated, not even a real person any more. Feelings of fear, dejection, non-existence came over him. He described what we call the night of the spirit. He went through this tremendous aridity for a year and a half. This was taking place at the time that I went to Gethsemani—the experience I described in the beginning of this chapter.

The "night of the spirit" is a time of purification and transformation. We become aware of our powerlessness, our capacity for evil, and a sense of abandonment by God. Powerlessness because no matter what we do it does not seem to help. The old ways of approaching things are ineffective. The depth of our selfishness and sinfulness is constantly before us. We realize that we could do these things again, even though we are aware of God's love for us. And of course there are periods of dryness, where it seems that God has abandoned us.

It is a period when the virtues of faith, hope, and charity really take root. Faith grows from just being a concept to a lived reality. Hope grows from being a attitude to a real trust in the walk of the Spirit to places we have never gone before. Charity moves from works to a union with all men and women in their joys and sorrows. In other words, faith, hope, and charity become more a part of our own being rather than a part of just our own philosophy and life.

What came out of this experience of the "night" was quite fruitful for Merton. In 1951 he became the master of scholastics, the beginning of fourteen years of involvement in the formation training of the young monks until 1965. Now when he talked about the spiritual journey, he could talk from his own inner truth. He said in 1951, "I am a new person. I have discovered what it means to be in the desert of compassion." He paid his dues of a year and a half of personal dryness. In the spiritual journey the only way to deal with a problem is to walk through it. We can't run away. There are no short-cuts. Merton's conferences to the young monks have been recorded and can be listened to today. From 1951 to 1955 he experienced a deep exhilaration at just being a father figure to these young men.

In 1955, although things were on an even keel in his life, he decided he wanted solitude. His yearning was so strong that he made a formal request for permission to transfer to the Camoldolese monastery in Frescati, Italy, where the monks lived as hermits. His abbot, however, was certain that it was God's will that Merton should remain at Gethsemani. Characterizing Merton as a fickle neurotic who didn't know his own mind, he persuaded the abbot general in Rome to insist that Merton remain at Gethsemani for five years with a moratorium on writing before any request for a transfer be considered.

At the end of 1955, his most difficult year, the third highest office at Gethsemani became vacant when the master of novices was elected abbot of another monastery. For reasons not entirely clear, Merton suggested himself for the job! Even more surprising, the abbot accepted his suggestion and appointed this "fickle neurotic." He gave this difficult job of forming young men's consciences as Trappists to this man whose stability and reliability he had been questioning! It pays never to try to figure the working of the hand of God. Some wonderful things happen even though the superior's motivation at times may not be the best.

Some important changes in attitude happened to Merton between 1955 and the early 1960s. He became aware that solitude was not necessarily having to be physically alone: it was possible to preserve inner solitude while being quite active.

He had a wonderful experience in March 1958 in Louisville (at the corner Walnut—now known as Mohammed Ali—and Fourth) while on the way to the doctor:

> I was suddenly overwhelmed with the realization that I loved all those people. They were mine and I, theirs. We could not be alien

to one another even though we were total strangers. It was like waking from a dream of separateness, of self-isolation in a special world, a world of renunciation and supposed holiness.

He realized there is no longer a "me" and a "you." On the spiritual journey we come to the realization that we are, in reality, "we." We are so connected that only illusion creates separateness. That was a breakthrough for Merton.

After this he became more involved in his writings with the topics of war and peace, disarmament, nonviolence, and interreligious dialogue. The yearning for solitude continued to grow. In 1960 a hermitage was built on the monastery grounds, and he received permission to spend short periods of time there. Finally in August of 1965, he formally entered the hermitage where he stayed until his death three years later.

> To remain in solitude is to remain in freedom and love of direct obedience to God and not withdrawing to the safety and security of a "tissue of works." I came into solitude to hear the word of God, to wait in expectation of a Christian fulfillment, to understand myself in relation to a community that doubts and questions itself and of which I am very much a part.

While at the hermitage Merton still had to deal with his struggles with regard to his abbot, in relationships with many friends, and especially a brief relationship he had with a young nurse. There were the tensions which arose out of his outspoken involvement with the peace and civil rights movements. And as always, the struggles within himself are reflected in his recently released journals. These struggles did not destroy his inner peace and joy of being a hermit. It was the "work" that solitude and silence demands of anyone who has the courage to enter its territory.

The storms which he experienced earlier of fornication, blasphemy, and dizziness, were now being experienced on a deeper level within himself; they now made him experience his powerlessness and thus deepened his faith, his trust, and gave him a greater sense of charity and love of the whole world.

This phase of personal conversion and spiritual espousal bore fruit and was manifested in many ways: freedom from the attraction of assuming a special role because of one's gifts and charism (he no longer clings to his role, his gifts, his talents; he lets them go); freedom from the domination by one's emotional programs that have been implanted from childhood (God has made him face his addictions, especially in affection and esteem, and reach out and claim God as his one and only source of fulfillment); a purification of one's ideas about God (as he opened more to the intimacy of God working in his life); a desire of self surrender to the will of God (knowing that he is called to more than just the keeping of the rule but to what the rule points to: discerning the will of God in his life); an awareness of God's infinite mercy (as he struggles with his interior demons and faces them with the help of God). All these are just facets of one person's desire and profound yearning to make an unconditional commitment to God.

Spiritual Marriage

Spiritual marriage has been described as a wound of consuming love. There is an experience or event where we are so overwhelmed by the presence of God that all else seems insignificant. It has been said to have three elements. The first is the death of the "false self," that illusion which we have of being outside the influence of God and on our own. Second, a greater empathy with the world in the sense that we are not only many but we are united as "one": "Whatever you do to the least, you do to me." Third, there is the acknowledgment that our being is being restructured on a deeper level. This awareness is not only intellectual but also an intuitive knowledge that defies analysis. Merton in his trip to Asia in 1968 had this type of experience that was abiding until his death.

His experience in Sri Lanka standing before the figures of the Buddha was one of a deep yearning, a spirit of abandonment, and yet a oneness with God and the world. This experience did not create any doubts in his mind and heart concerning his Christian roots and vocation, but instead deepened what he was and brought clarity to what he believed. We may sometimes have a deeper experience of God outside of our own tradition: it may not cause us to leave our faith, but it puts a new life into our faith. It makes us see all that we believed and lived in a new way:

> Looking at these figures I was suddenly, almost forcibly, jerked clear out of the habitual, the half-tied vision of things, and an inner clearness, clarity, as if exploding from the rocks themselves, became evident and obvious. . . . I don't know when in my life I have ever had such a sense of beauty and spiritual validity running together in one aesthetic illumination . . . my Asian pilgrimage has come clear and purified itself . . . I don't know what else remains but I have now seen and have pierced through the surface and have got beyond the shadow and the disguise.

Merton has experienced the overwhelming presence of God. This reminds me of the story that is told of St. Thomas Aquinas when he had an experience of God: he wanted to burn all his writings because they were like straw in comparison to who God really is. It is an experience one never forgets.

Personal Death

Then came Merton's tragic accidental death a few weeks later on December 10, 1968, in Bangkok, Thailand, after delivering an address to a monastic gathering calling for greater dialogue among world religious leaders for the sake of peace. With death came the final meeting with God, Who had been working with and on Merton from the time of his creation in the womb and even before. I see death as the Lord squeezing us until our false self is let go of and then filling us with the richness of our true self who is our God.

I have shared Merton's story with you because I believe it is an excellent example of what the spiritual journey is all about. The importance of interior silence in our lives does not distance us from the world but makes us one with the whole world.

Merton is an example of the rough rhythms of the journey. We don't go from confusion to clarity, from chaos to neatness. We fall apart periodically as part of the journey. We come together in newness. That's the way it's supposed to be. We get squeezed until we are empty so we can be filled with God. Our love relationship with God could be more accurately described as arm-wrestling. We struggle and strain until we give up and then win. That is what happened to Jacob when he lost the wrestling match with the angel, but gained the blessing of God.

Just look back on our lives, what we have been through, what we have survived. Can we not see how God has been working in our lives through the various thresholds? Why would a God who has been with us through the years not be with us at this time in our lives? My dad used to say to me, "There are times that God really slams the door in our face, with such force that when we turn our heads, we see that the force of the slam opened up two other doors." Have you not experienced that in your life? Thomas Keating describes conversion as changing the way we look for happiness in our lives. In a sense, turning our heads and seeing what else God has in store for us.

I hope you will explore Thomas Merton's writings more fully, especially, *The Seven Storey Mountain, New Seeds of Contemplation,* and *The Wisdom of the Desert.* I also highly recommend Basil Pennington's work *Thomas Merton, Brother Monk,* published by Harper and Row.

As I said in the beginning of this chapter, I believe that the life of Thomas Merton can serve as a working model for the spiritual journey. By working model, I do not mean only the details of his life but the movements that took place in his life. The stages or thresholds that he experienced are in many ways not unlike what we go through in our own way. Nobody's saying that Merton was perfect. He wasn't. That's one of the reasons he is so attractive to contemporary people. He was on a journey. He was alive. He was deeply human. He was profoundly spiritual. He consented to God's presence and action in his life.

5 ❀

The Lectio Divina *Tradition: Lost and Found*

One of the great treasures of the Christian tradition of prayer has a Latin name, *lectio divina*, which literally means divine reading: reading Scriptures in order to make them part of one's life. This tradition of prayer flows out of a Hebrew method of studying the Scriptures called *haggadah*. It was an interactive interpretation of the Scriptures by means of the free use of the text to explore their inner meaning. It was part of the devotional practice of the Jews in the days of Jesus. The Jews would memorize the text in a process that involved repeating the passage over and over softly with the lips until the words themselves gradually took up residence in the heart, there transforming the person's life. There is a phrase that captures the spirit of this practice— "learning by heart." The repetition of the words began to have an impact on the whole being, most especially the heart.

The Christian approach to the Scriptures is deeply rooted in this Hebrew method but takes on its own style.

Let me make a point of clarification. There are two traditional approaches to *lectio divina*: the monastic and the scholastic. The *monastic* version goes back to around the fourth century. It applies to a particular way in which the monks prayed on their own throughout the day. When they would gather to pray the

Liturgy of the Hours with the community during the day, a particular Scripture phrase might catch a monk's attention: he would then hold on to it and carry it with him during the day ruminating over it—"a gentle chewing" which might lead to spontaneous prayer and a resting in the power of the word. Although there are different "moments" in the prayer, it does not follow a set order: it is fluid; it goes with the flow of the spirit in a *receptive* way. The word becomes part of the monk himself and plays a very important role as he goes about the activities of the day. For the sake of clarity when I am speaking about the various movements in this monastic *lectio,* I will refer to them as the *four moments* of prayer.

The other approach to *lectio divina* is called the *scholastic.* This came out of the writings of Guigo the Carthusian in the twelfth century. Please remember that this was a time in the Church when a more analytical approach was used in writing about spiritual matters. Therefore Guigo took the four "moments" and analyzed them and put them in a systematic order, thus describing what was going on during the various moments of monastic *lectio.* It is a more *concentrative* approach. I must say in all fairness, that Guigo never intended that these four moments be seen as separate elements or parts of *lectio*—parts which would stand on their own. But this is what happened during the centuries after his work. In the spirit of what has developed when we speak of scholastic *lectio divina,* I will refer to the *four steps.*

No matter which approach we use, both methods of *lectio* lead to the same place: a deeper and more profound encounter with the Word of God. It so happens that once the Scripture is read, one approach is more receptive and the other more concentrative; one is fluid and the other more programmed. One is seemingly more open to the movement of the Spirit and the other is caught up in the steps of the practice. Both lead to an opening to the contemplative dimension of the gospel.

It has been my experience that it is best to begin with the scholastic approach. This way the various moments and steps of the prayer can be learned. They can be used in community prayer even thought the practice was designed for individual prayer time.

For the sake of clarity I will use the word "moments" when discussing the monastic approach to *lectio divina* and the word "steps" in talking about the scholastic. The important issue is to pray and to encounter the power of the Holy Spirit in Scripture.

Having said all of this in preparation, let me walk you through the scholastic approach. In a sense let me teach you what I like to call the four-step dance of prayer. Once one appreciates the steps of the prayer then the moments make more sense.

Lectio divina is really a four-step discipline built around the practice of reading Scripture. The *lectio divina* tradition can be deceptive. Guigo the Carthusian comes with an intuitive insight that simplifies these four steps of the prayer. His insights make a lot of sense today, when people like to have a "how to" approach. Guigo was, in a sense, ahead of his time, almost prophetic in the way he presented the practice.

Guigo called the exercise *The Ladder of the Monks* by which one may ascend up from earth to heaven, as on Jacob's ladder. It allows us to move up and down, skip steps, take detours and in general move freely. It is important, however, that four rungs be part of the life of this tradition (italics are mine):

> *Reading* directs the mind to a careful looking at the Scriptures. *Meditation* is the studious activity of the mind, pondering the knowledge of some hidden truth under the guidance of our own reason. *Prayer* is a devout turning of the heart to God to get ills removed and to obtain good things. *Contemplation* is a certain elevation above itself of the mind which is suspended in God, tasting the joy of eternal sweetness.

The first rung is *reading* (*lectio* is the Latin word for reading). It directs us to carefully listening to the Scriptures. This reminds me of Eastern rite masses and the chant that is heard before the reading of the Gospel: "Be attentive, be attentive." The congregation is called to a listening that is deep and attentive.

The second stage is *meditation* (the Latin for this step is *meditatio*). This second rung is the studious activity of the mind, probing the meaning of and application to the text to our lives under the guidance of the Spirit working with our intellect. This stage has been also called discursive meditation.

The third stage is called *prayer* (the Latin for this is *oratio*). Guigo describes prayer as the devout turning of the heart to God to get ills removed or to obtain good things. It is intercessory prayer or affective prayer. Praying from, with and through our hearts.

The final stage is *contemplation* (the Latin term is *contemplatio*). It is a resting in the power of the word of God. He describes contemplation as a "certain elevation of the mind above itself which is suspended in God, tasting the joy of eternal sweetness."

Earlier in the book I discussed this term "contemplation." It can be acquired or infused. When it is acquired, then our initiative brings about the resting; if it is infused, then a gift from the spirit brings on a even deeper resting—a resting that is beyond our ability to do on our own. Here I am speaking of a resting in the power of the Word of God; it is another form of acquired contemplation.

Scholastic *lectio* is Guigo's gift to us. He goes on to say:

> I sought your face, O Lord, your face, O Lord have I sought it. I have long meditated in my heart and in my meditation a fire grew with a desire to know you more. While you broke the bread of sacred Scripture for me you have become known to me in the breaking of the bread. The more I know you, the more I long to know you, no longer in the husks of the letter but in senses of experience.

Many people, earnest people of devout prayer, settle for husks. When Guigo talks about contemplation and describes how it can take over in one's life, he writes:

> While the soul is calling for the Lord like this, yearning, God does not wait until the soul is finished speaking but interrupts the flow of prayer in mid-course and hastens to present himself. He comes to meet the yearning soul bathed with the dew of heavenly sweetness, drenched in the finest perfume. He strengthens the weary soul and refreshes it in its hunger. He fertilizes its dryness, makes it forget earthly things, marvelously bringing it to life by mortifying it in forgetfulness. He makes the soul forget itself and makes it sober by inebriating it.

This is the kernel beneath the husks. When the soul is in contemplation, the prayer effort is interrupted by the overpowering effortless grace of God. The person praying may not even know this is happening. Our structures, concepts, and images all disappear. When Guigo writes about the forgetfulness of self that takes place, this is what he refers to. So when *The Cloud of Unknowing* is written (to be discussed in chapter 7), it is referring to this tradition of forgetting, of *not* knowing. Guigo has to resort to paradox to explain the loss and gain. He writes that grace, the presence of God, makes the soul sober by inebriating it:

> He who humbles himself shall be exalted and he who exalts himself shall be humbled. What we must do and can not do is done for us without our knowledge of it having been done, lest we fall into the trap of trying to achieve what only can be done without effort, as an outright gift.

When we decide that this is as much as we are going to have, because we want to stay sober, then the Spirit introduces us to drunkenness and confusion. We become like St. Peter at Pentecost: we face the charge of drunkenness. Do you remember how the crowd said that the disciples must be drunk when they received the Holy Spirit? But here, if we drink our fill, we pass through drunkenness to clarity. These words do not make sense on a literal level. Much of Scripture and religious language is "short circuited" because we hold on to the literal and don't let the poetic move us to a deeper understanding.

Guigo sums this up in another way:

> Reading is, at it were, the foundation and comes first. It supplies material and then refers us to meditation. Meditation earnestly inquires what we should seek and as it were, digs out and finds the treasures and shows us the treasures. But since it cannot obtain anything by itself, [because the head can never get us where we want to go], it refers us to prayer. Prayer raises itself up with all its might toward God and asks for the desired treasure, the sweetness of contemplation. This, when it comes, rewards the labors of the preceding three.

I like to share a story which comes to mind as I read this phrase, "Prayer raises itself up with all its might toward God and asks for the desired treasure." A number of years ago I was with a group of friends in northern California, taking a self-guided tour of one of the redwood forest groves. One of the signs indicated that the redwood tree has the vast majority of its branches on the top because it is struggling with the other trees to get as much sun as possible and be able to grow taller. In our group was a woman of small dimensions physically but a giant in personality. She stopped, planted her feet on the ground, raised her hands stretching upward as high as she could proclaiming, "Grow, grow, I want to be like the redwood tree." It was a sight I shall never forget. This is us. We know that we are little but we want to be a giant in the eyes of God by the depth of our yearning for God because God is our desired treasure.

Guigo issues a gentle warning that it is important to be faithful to all four steps:

> Reading without meditation is arid. Meditation without reading is erroneous. Prayer without meditation is tepid. Meditation without prayer is fruitless. Prayer with devotion wins contemplation, but the attainment of contemplation without prayer is rare and miraculous.

So here is *lectio divina* in the contemplative dimension. We need all four steps as we progress in our journey. There are times when we will put more effort into the reading; others, into reflecting. There are times when we are moved more to affective prayer and other times to resting. All four steps are always there but the Spirit moves us at time to emphasis one more than the others until we learn the dance. We need all four for real nourishment. If we are conscious of this whole process being present, then the prayer is enriching and fruitful.

Let me tell you a story. When I was a young priest I was assigned to Little Flower parish. One of the couples in the parish were part-time dance instructors at an Arthur Murray Dance Studio, a famous chain throughout the country. The couple approached the pastor and offered, as a money-maker for the parish, to give dance lessons to our married couples, twice a year for six weeks, one night a week. The pastor said yes. Let me tell you what a sight it was to see married couples learning some new dances. It was not an easy process, but by the end of each evening, it was also quite a sight to see how well they looked when they finally got it. The point of the story is that if they were to be able to move beyond their ordinary habit of dance they had to take the time to learn something new. Step by step by step, until it was not just a series of steps but became a "dance." You have to learn the steps before you can move into the moments of dance. As this applies to dance, it also applies to *lectio divina*.

The four steps constitute a single exercise or movement. Guigo does not call the steps exercises; he sees them as four components of one entity, one exercise. Remember from the beginning that the purpose of the exercise is to open us to the presence and action of God within us. The four steps are a continuum that are to continually nourish us by keeping us aware of the presence of God. In many presentations of the exercise, the four steps are so distinct and analytical that one gets the impression that there are four kinds of prayers. Could each step be taken as a separate prayer practice? Of course. But this betrays the genius of the prayer. This is what has happened since Guigo's time. This analytical approach is a good tool for understanding, but the danger is that we will miss the dynamic character of the total exercise.

Let me make one more comment. I know the *lectio divina* was always looked upon in the tradition as being done individually. I, however, believe that there is a contemporary development taking place. More and more of our Centering Prayer groups have from the beginning, now well over fifteen years, shared *lectio divina*. *Lectio divina* was done in common after the group had prayed Centering Prayer. The idea was that out of the silence, the Word of God is heard on a much deeper level and with greater openness. The Scripture is read three or four times and the group sharing is done either after each step or at the end of the fourth step after the closing prayer. The sharings are always brief. There is a great value in the community experience. Yes, it is not *lectio* as it was presented traditionally, but I believe it is a new development of the tradition to meet the needs of contemporary people, as was the development of Centering Prayer. For that reason I do not call it "praying the Scriptures" but *lectio divina* in common.

I recommend Simon Tugwell's book, *Ways of Imperfection,* for those who want to go more in depth into the historical background of *lectio divina*.

This process of *lectio divina* was not always well understood, at least not in this way. Guigo came forward with his "ladder of the monks" in the middle of the twelfth century. Without going into detail, let me recall for you that for much of our tradition, the two things necessary for devotion were prayer and reading of Scripture or commentaries on it. Most of the time, the emphasis was on constant reading. In the fifth century St. Benedict, father of monasticism in the West, made specific time in his rule for spiritual reading. His rule was highly influential throughout the centuries. He did not set any time aside for meditative prayer, his emphasis was on communal prayer in the Divine Office. Private or personal prayer was to be "brief and frequent."

The assumption was that one prayed in short spurts throughout the day, but to keep one's mind in tune with the tradition, the Church, and the mind of Christ, one was supposed to do much reading. Tugwell tells a charming story of St. Leoba, a close friend of St. Boniface, a Benedictine who became a missionary to the Germanic tribes of the eighth century. This was said of her:

> She applied herself with such diligence to reading that unless she was given time for prayer or her frail body was given food or sleep, the sacred page never fell from her hand. She even had the custom of having the Bible read to her during her sleep! The younger girls took up this task and it seemed a bit unusual because if they skipped a single syllable, she corrected them from her sleep!

St. Ambrose says of Origen, one of the most learned of the early Church fathers, that food was never taken except in the presence of reading. At bedtime, one of the brethren had to recite some of the sacred texts. Origen's view was that this practice, both day and night, assured that prayer always followed reading and reading always followed prayer.

This extreme emphasis on reading prevails to our day. On retreat, some people read during the whole time. In fact as I look back on some of my earlier retreat notes, I can now confess that I was doing "book reports" on the books I read during the retreat. The sad fact was that I read them as an intellectual exercise. I believe that the more I knew the better my life would be. True to a point, but then these words had to touch my heart for the journey to continue. I can see now that it was a way of not really surrendering my control to the Spirit. No harm done. When the time is right, then we see what we need to see.

In summary we might say that for much of our history, reading was encouraged, prayer was on our own, and meditation was considered primarily an intellectual exercise (or later, an affective exercise using the imagination). Contemplation always seemed to be misunderstood or was not taken seriously as part of the normal development of prayer, at least for ordinary folks. So the steps of scholastic *lectio divina* were to read, to reflect, to respond, and to rest. The Latin term for these steps are *lectio, meditatio, oratio,* and *contemplatio.* For all too long the emphasis remained on the *lectio* and the *meditatio.* It is only in recent times that the *oratio* and *contemplatio* have been coming into their own in the prayer life of everyday people.

The monastic *lectio divina* is much like the scholastic except in two areas. First, it is not seen as being a set form of prayer but rather as moments experienced throughout the day. A word or phrase is taken into the daily activity, where sometimes it will be thought about, other times it will be prayed over, and other times one will simply rest in the power of the word. It is receptive and fluid and washes over one throughout the day. The second difference is in the second step. In the scholastic it is *meditatio,* a pondering, a reflecting on the word, an engaging the intellect. In the monastic is it *ruminatio,* a gentle chewing, savoring, a gentle being with the word or phrase; it does not engage the intellect. This is a subtle, yet important, difference. Experience has shown that it helps one to move more into the contemplative dimension of the gospel. How? By moving one toward the heart rather than the intellect.

It is my opinion that we first learn the scholastic so that we can understand the steps, then move gently into the monastic, where we move into the moments. Again it is like learning how to dance: There we are on the dance floor. We have learned some new steps. As the music is playing we are concentrating on how our feet are moving. After a while we get comfortable with the steps and begin to listen to the music. We not only listen but we are swept up into it. The steps become moments of the dance—no longer steps of a dance, but *moments* in the dance.

Let me share the comments of Thomas Keating on the monastic form of *lectio*:

> It is the most ancient and was practiced by the Mothers and Fathers of the Desert and later in monasteries both in the east and the west. It is orientated more toward contemplative prayer than the scholastic form, especially when the latter developed into what we call today discursive meditation, conceived as moving from one thought to another or as one stage in a series of steps. That method is a good way of praying provided you don't get stuck there and fail to move to contemplative prayer. In the monastic there are no stages, ladders or steps but there are moments.

One moment feeds the other. We open the text of Scripture and take a phrase with us into the activities of the day, holding that phrase, perhaps praying over it, or just being with it. We allow the Scripture phrase to enter more deeply into our being. The phrase is carried with us throughout the day and at various times we will have a moment with the phrase. It becomes so much a part of us that it is like our breathing. That is why an understanding of *lectio* is important to an understanding of the role of Centering Prayer itself.

Bringing the Prayer into Daily Life

There is another aspect of this tradition that I should mention. Hugh of St. Victor, who wrote fifty years before Guigo, said there also needs to be a step called *operatio*. Hugh was concerned that people who prayed would not see the value of putting their prayer into action. I have always believed that genuine prayer leads to genuine concern and action and genuine action leads back to prayer. It seems that Guigo did not want to include *operatio* because it tended to break the rhythm of his schema. He is right, but it is helpful to see the connection with everyday life.

It would make sense that in the fourfold exercise of *lectio divina* we eventually enter into silence and from the energy of that silence we explode out into action in the world—the *operatio.* Work throws us back not on our resources, which are always inadequate, but back to relying on the strength of God. So we turn to prayer to accomplish what we want in that *operatio.* William Shannon, in his book, *Seeking the Face of God,* has a marvelous chapter on *operatio.* He makes the term current and calls it social action.

A fine theologian, Robert Mulholland, Jr., in studying John Wesley, indicates another tradition that developed after Guigo. He describes this rhythm: First there is silence. Out of the silence comes the reading. Out of the reading comes listening or meditation. Out of that comes prayer and from prayer we move to contemplation. He says that contemplation leads naturally to what he calls *incarnatio,* the enfleshing of prayer energy. He substitutes *incarnatio* for the word *operatio.* The understanding is that when we become close to the Word in prayer, we enflesh that Word in our lives. The Incarnation that started with Jesus continues in us. Then our social action is an acting out of what we have experienced in prayer. The action is done with a spirit of compassion and openness.

We all have realized in our experience that after we work for any length of time, we become aware of a not-so-subtle need for peace and quiet. Only it isn't just peace and quiet, it is the resting in the Lord. We've all said, "I just need a little peace and quiet" at times in our life. Simple rest will help us with fatigue, but what we really long for is the deeper rest we achieve in prayer.

This rhythmic sequence makes it impossible for prayer time to be isolated. We just don't say, "We are now going to pray." Our *life* is prayer. The integration of prayer into this moving sequence works quite well for most folks. Prayer can be integrated into the unstructured business that marks the way most people spend the time and energy of their lives.

Return to the Lectio Divina Tradition

Why does this discussion of the prayer seem so new ? How did we lose it, so to speak? Historically, this loss happened because of four situations. First, the Reformation of the sixteenth century caused the Church to tighten up and back away from the affective and contemplative dimension—the *oratio* and *contemplatio*. These were difficulties to control and the Church was looking for more control during those turbulent times. Whenever the Church feels threatened, it goes to her head and leaves behind the heart. I know this is a simple observation concerning a complex question, but I believe it sums it up in a "nutshell": clearer rules, more detailed catechisms, more frequent pronouncements, and tighter surveillance on all sides. This is fine, but not to the detriment of the freedom to pursue the contemplative dimension.

This attitude was intensified, not by St. Ignatius, who was quite aware of the power of affective prayer and contemplation, but by lesser lights in the community who felt they had to tighten up his spiritual exercises. They came to play down the affective and contemplative aspect. It is only recently that critical studies have been done on the Spiritual Exercises. What are these Spiritual Exercises of St. Ignatius formulated in the sixteenth century? They are a process and formula of retreat and reflection to help a person make a commitment to Christ and the Church. It is one of the most popular approaches to the spiritual journey.

Then a heresy called Quietism arose. There is quite a bit of controversy historically about this heresy, which seemed to imply that all other responsibilities were taken care of as long as your heart was in the right place. So you didn't have to worry about listening and meditation and reading. Whatever you did was pleasing to God because you had given God your whole heart. Some interpretations created problems, so the Church condemned the heresy.

Later there was Jansenism. This heresy was reluctant to talk about the immanence of God. It was darkly suspicious of human goodness and suggested that merit was needed to win God's love. That made the emphasis on study, right thinking, and asceticism even greater. How can people be comfortable with the rudderless journey of contemplation when their emotions and instincts are questionable at best? Unless they "thought" carefully, they could really get into trouble. The emphasis was on reading, meditation, and the making of resolutions. Once again, fine, but what happened to the rest of the story, affective prayer and contemplation?

About this time, devotionalism and the cult of the saints became very popular. Number symbolism also became important. Seven of this and twelve of that and nine of lots more things. I'm not critical of this approach, but it is incomplete. It leaves out some rungs of the monk's ladder.

So how did *lectio divina* revive? After World War II, the charismatic movement emphasized affective prayer a great deal. People began to discover there could be room for heart, feelings, and emotions in prayer. The charismatic movement crossed over all church boundaries, touching them in different ways. So we did what we always do: we went back into our tradition to see if we have this emphasis. Yes, we do. We lost it and now we found it again—*oratio,* affective prayer.

I remember the first time that I encountered a charismatic prayer group. It was school policy to encourage the use of the parish school at night by various groups and organizations. I was walking through our school. Out of one of the classrooms I heard all this singing and praying in "strange sounds." I said to myself, "What in God's name is this?" I have come to realize they were "*oratio*-ing"—praying from their hearts. They were praying the third step—affective prayer.

After Vatican II, when the major contemplative orders were asked by the Holy Father Pope Paul VI to rediscover their charism, they went back to their historical roots and become more aware of the contemplative dimension. They acknowledged that some or perhaps most of that contemplative dimension had become lost or at least diminished in the business of running the convents and monasteries in this modern world. They began to rediscover the beauty of the contemplative practice.

In the 1970s leaders like Carmelite Ernest Larkin, Benedictine Father John Main, the Trappists Basil Pennington, Thomas Keating, William Meninger, and others (George Maloney, William Green, William Johnson) began actively to teach the contemplative tradition. In the beginning there were two reactions. Some thought they were on the fringe. How could this be our Christian tradition? Others were immediately taken by the teaching, for they were experiencing quiet and silence in their prayer time and did not know what was happening. And so by the persistence and goodness of these men and others, we rediscovered this contemplative dimension of prayer as well as the contemplative dimension of *lectio divina*.

Beyond their efforts, what also helped us realize that we had lost two rungs of the ladder (the affective and contemplative) was post-Vatican II scholarship. We began to have access to the actual texts of St. John of the Cross and St. Teresa of Ávila. The poor Carmelites! They had to clip, cut, edit, and amend their documents in order to get through the sixteenth-century Inquisition. We never had their complete written documents. But after World War II, we began to have access to the unedited texts. For the first time in centuries, we could study what they really said and meant in full. We discovered these and other superstars of our tradition, as well as the Church fathers. Now our new (yet traditional and ancient) understanding was that not only was contemplative prayer for a few specific religious orders, it was for all people and part of the tradition of the universal Church. The whole tradition had a contemplative component.

At the same time something was happening in our culture. The hunger for contemplation was such that hundreds and thousands of Catholics were leaving the Church and going to the East to learn prayer and spirituality. The Church had never taught them how to pray! They had been taught prayers, but not how to pray. Prayer in parish life seldom went beyond moral exhortation and post-Reformation devotions. Catholics were flocking to TM, to Buddhism, to Zen—whoever would teach them to pray! These traditions have marvelous meditation practices that have stood the test of time.

But we had nothing to offer these seekers. So when Larkin, Main, Pennington, Meninger, and Keating began to give workshops on contemplation, people came from all directions and persuasions. When they went to dialogue with the Hindu and Buddhist practitioners they realized that half of the audience was Roman Catholic, 40 percent were Jewish, and 10 percent were "others."

Both Catholic and Jewish traditions had stirred up in their people a desire for closeness with God and then were not able to tell them or show them how to enter into that union. The people wanted the experience of contemplation—that much was clear. Books and tapes on the topic were becoming best-sellers.

I am not well-known in the workshop world, but when I conduct a workshop on *lectio divina*, contemplation, and Centering Prayer, hundreds of people attend. People's hearts have been opened and they are eager to learn about the journey to which we are all called. It is important to emphasize that we are discovering our own tradition. This is not new: it is not peripheral, it is not a threat to existing piety. It is simply the fullness of our tradition.

Our challenge is to help people make this tumultuous journey and not get stuck. People want the contemplative journey, but it cannot be taken lightly. That's why Guigo's teaching is so helpful—he gives us some kind of structure and conceptual background to build on. It helps to know there is a blueprint and a map as we enter into that mysterious world of prayer and silence.

Perhaps a well-worn story in a new context will summarize the genius of the *lectio divina*. A Baptist minister was asked the secret of his inspiring sermons. Not given to theological abstraction, he answered eloquently, "I read myself full, I think myself clear, I pray myself hot, then I let myself go." That's an accurate summary of the process we've just described.

I believe St. John of the Cross has this saying. "Seek in reading, and you will find in meditation. Knock in prayer and it will be opened to you in contemplation."

Dom Marmion, the famous French Benedictine, says, "We read under the eye of God until the heart is touched and leaps to flame." We read (*lectio*), under the eye of God (*meditatio*) until the heart is touched (*oratio*) and leaps to flame (*contemplatio*).

Role of Centering Prayer

Centering Prayer is distinct from *lectio* but part of the family of prayer. It is a communion with God and also a discipline. Later we will cover some of these details but for now let me say this: Centering Prayer helps us detach from overconceptualization, hyperactivity, and overdependence on self. It makes room for the gift of contemplation. But at the same time it helps us let go of overconcern about our own way of thinking, the desire to prove our worth by our activity and not by our presence, and at times an attitude that we can do all things on our own. When we let go of these attitudes there is created in us a deep place for the word of God to enter as we take the time to pray *lectio divina*. The *lectio* reminds us of whom we rest with in the silence of Centering Prayer.

Role of Lectio Divina *with Other Prayers and Spiritual Reading*

I have found it quite helpful to apply the steps and moments of *lectio* to my traditional prayers. When I conduct parish missions I use the Hail Mary as an example of applying the four steps. It opens for people the possibilities of praying the prayers that they already know at a deeper level. I have also used it when reading some of the spiritual classics. To take a paragraph from John of the Cross and read it four times applying the appropriate question to each of the readings helps to get past the husks of the words and into the kernel. The *lectio divina* tradition has many applications for the contemporary pilgrim on this spiritual journey.

Practical Suggestions

Please remember that *lectio divina* is a private prayer practice, done individually at a suitable time. It does not follow any discipline but opens itself to the action of the Holy Spirit. Please read carefully the following examples of scholastic and monastic *lectio divina* designed to be done in group. This is not only a concession but I believe a new movement of the Spirit to a growing number of people who have a hunger to share the Scriptures in this way. I have also included an example for private *lectio*.

If you are going to use the scholastic approach, then you might think in terms of reading, reflecting, responding, and resting in the Word of God. If you are going to use the monastic, you may want to think in terms of reading, ruminating, responding, and resting, and being the Word of God.

A Scholastic Method of Lectio Divina for Community Prayer

1. Lectio: (Listening to the Word of God or Reading God's Word)

As we listen to the Word of God for the first time, I invite you to be aware of any word or phrase that catches your attention.

Read the passage slowly with appropriate pauses.

Allow one minute of silence for reflection

Ask the listeners to share out loud with the whole group if they are moved to do so—what was the word or phrase that caught their attention in the reading?

After the sharing, allow a few moments of silence in order that what was heard may sink deeper within.

2. Meditatio: (Reflecting on the Word of God)

As we listen to the Word of God for the second time I invite you to be aware of any reflection or thought that you become aware of as you listened—a reflection or thought.

Read the passage slowly with appropriate pauses.

Allow one minute of silence for reflection

Ask the listeners to share out loud with the whole group if they are moved to do so—what reflection or thought did they become aware of as they listened?

After the sharing, allow a few moments of silence in order that what was heard may sink deeper within.

3. Oratio: (Responding to the Word of God)—Affective Prayer

As we listen to the Word of God for a third time, I invite you to be aware of any prayer that rises up within you that expresses what you are experiencing in this Word of God.

Read the passage slowly with appropriate pauses.

Allow one minute of silence for reflection.

Ask the listeners to share out loud with the whole group if they are moved to do so—a prayer that expresses what they are experiencing in this Word of God.

After the sharing allow a few moments of silence in order that what was heard may sink deeper within.

4. Contemplatio: (Resting in the Word of God)—Contemplation

As we listen to the Word of God for a fourth time, I invite you to just sit with the Word of God and allow God to speak to you in the silence of your hearts. God's first language is silence.

Read the passage slowly with appropriate pauses.

Allow three or four minutes of silence.

Closing Prayer: Almighty God, thank you for the gift of your Word. May we take the word or phrase that spoke to us, the thought that we became aware of, and the prayer that came from our hearts into the activity of our day (the time of this retreat) as a reminder of our genuine desire to consent to your presence and action in our lives. We pray this prayer through Jesus Christ, Our Lord. Amen

Gently ring the bell to end the session and leave in silence.

A Monastic Method of Lectio Divina for Community Prayer

Preliminary Comments: The monastic way is unstructured, in a sense methodless. One reads or listens to the word of God and then the only process is to follow the attraction of the Spirit.

For example:

• As you listen, you may be aware of the phrase, sentence, or even one word that catches your attention (reading);

• or sit with the phrase, sentence, or word, repeating it gently over and over in you heart, not thinking about it but just being with it (ruminating);

• or be aware of any prayer that rises up within you that expresses what you are experiencing in this Word of God (responding);

• or just rest in the phrase, sentence, or even one word, resting with God beyond your thoughts and reflections in the power of His Word (resting).

Read the passage slowly (with appropriate pauses) a number of times.

Allow one and a half to three minutes of silence after each reading.

Closing Prayer: Almighty God, thank you for the gift of resting with your Word. May we take the phrase, sentence, or even one word that spoke to us and the prayer that came from our hearts into the activity of our day as a reminder of our genuine desire to consent to your presence and action in our lives. We pray that we may become this Word through Jesus Christ, Our Lord. Amen

Optional: After the closing prayer, ask the participants to join in a brief faith sharing that expresses what they are experiencing with the Word of God. After the sharing, allow a few moments of silence in order that what was heard may sink more deeply within.

Gently ring the bell to end the silence

The Private Practice of Lectio Divina

1. Read the Scripture passage for the first time. (It helps to read it aloud softly.) What phrase, sentence, or even one word stands out to you? Begin to repeat that phrase, sentence, or word over and over, allowing it to settle deeply in your heart. Do any insights begin to arise? Do not expand these insights right now; this can be done at a later time. Simply return to the repetition of the phrase, sentence, or even one word, savoring it in your heart.

2. Relish these words; let them resound in your heart. Read the passage as often as you wish, learning these words by heart as you continue to repeat them in your mind.

3. Let an attitude of quiet receptiveness permeate the prayer time, an openness to a deeper hearing of the Word of God.

4. As you continue to "listen" to this phrase, sentence, or even one word, a prayer may arise spontaneously in response. Offer that prayer, then return to repeating the word in your heart.

5. When you find that you move beyond the meaning of the phrase, sentence, or word to the gift of the divine presence of the Word, rest in God as long as the Presence or attraction remains.

Note: These steps are not separate, but flow into each other. There is no hurry to finish any particular chapter or verse; it is more important to listen deeply to God's word to you at this moment.

To extend the practice: After the resting, take the phrase, sentence, or word into your daily activity and listen to it, reflect on it, pray over it, and rest in it as time allows during the day. Allow it to become part of you.

6 ❀

The Method of
Centering Prayer

The ideal way to learn Centering Prayer is by attending an all-day introductory workshop sponsored by Contemplative Outreach. General information for doing so is available in the back of the book. Of course, in saying this am I showing my preference? There are other approaches to teaching Centering Prayer. However, as you have noticed already and will see in some of the following chapters, Centering Prayer is set in a conceptual background which is necessary for a fuller understanding of the spiritual journey. So I feel nothing beats the workshop experience. I have had been told by people who have read all the books on Centering Prayer that after attending a workshop, they realized they had not properly understood the practice.

I also ask you to refer to the appendix "The Method of Centering Prayer" by Thomas Keating, which we use at the introductory workshops.

Centering Prayer is both a relationship and a discipline.

Why do I say a relationship? Because when we say, "Let us pray," we are saying let us have a relationship with God. It is not just a communication of words; it is a communication between beings, one finite and the other infinite. I use this expression "relationship" because I believe it captures the profoundness of the dynamic of prayer. Let me explore with you this concept of prayer as relationship.

As we looked at the four steps or moments of *lectio divina*, it was much like a relationship: to read, to reflect, to respond, to rest, indicating ever-deepening levels of relationship with the Word of God. When we look at human relationships, we also can see ever deepening levels of intimacy with one another. We can see four levels in relationship there as well: acquaintance, friendliness, friendship and union. Let's examine these for a moment and then see how they apply to *lectio* and to prayer in general.

Relationship on the *acquaintance* level: here people are just getting to know one another. There is an exchange of basic information. At times the conversation is simply a monologue. It could be said, we are talking *at* each other: there is a listening quality to the exchange, but there isn't a connection or a flow to the conversation.

As the relationship grows a *friendliness* begins to develop. In terms of conversation there is an interest in what is being said; there is an exchange of ideas and concerns, but very rarely is there any sharing in depth.

We exchange ideas, we respect one another, we influence one another—the connection is real and lasting. The dialogue is a reflective process in which a person looks at things from a variety of points of view. We are not just talking *at* one another, but there is a inner conversation going on as well. It is good, solid surface material; in a sense it is the laying of the foundation for friendship.

The friendliness begins to blossom into *friendship* when the conversation becomes a deeper dialogue. In friendship, sometimes we talk at one another, sometimes we exchange ideas, work things out with each other, but then there are times when there is a mutual sharing of intimate things about each other. I like to picture it as an opening of the tabernacle of our heart to each other. This sharing is received with respect: there is no danger of it being thrown back into our face when we are angry at each other. There is no danger of it being shared with other people inappropriately. When this level of trust has been reached, it is possible to feel deep affection and caring for each other.

That's real friendship. We can't have a lot of friends like that. It takes energy to have good friends and we are doubly blessed to have a few in our lifetime.

The final level of relationship is *union*. Two people feel so united to each other that it is transforming. Picture two elderly people sitting on the porch together in silence. Rocking back and forth. Married for years. Wasting time together. They've done the monologue, the dialogue, the sharing of affection and friendship. Now they don't have to do anything. They are part of each other. Perhaps that's what we all want, to grow old in union with God. In fact it is said that after many years of marriage, couples begin to look like each other. Why? Because they have shared so much that one might say, "They have rubbed off on one another."

Here is the point I want to emphasize. As there are steps and moments in *lectio divina* and levels in relationship, these apply to prayer in general. Let me put it this way—show me how you pray and you show me how much intimacy you want with God. If you just say your prayers each day, then you are on an acquaintance level with God. If you not only say your prayers each day, but also reflect on what you are saying, then you are on a friendliness level with God. If you say you prayers, reflect on them, but also respond from your heart, then you are on a friendship level with God. And if you do all of these three in the course of your prayer and then also rest with God, like the elderly couple—waste time with God in silence—then you are on a union level with God. Show me how you pray and you are showing me how much intimacy you want with God. Does that make sense?

Our God will never be accused of spiritual harassment. God waits for us to express the level of intimacy that we want. God pushes and hints to us to have a deeper desire, but God will never force Himself on us. Our prayer level sends a sign to God concerning which level we are on and how much we open ourselves to intimacy.

Now we have been taught how to read and how to reflect; we are beginning to know how to respond, but we have not been taught how to rest, to simply be. The practice of *lectio divina* is one way of developing a relationship with God; these four steps or moments are not unlike the four levels of relationship. But when it comes to just simply resting in the presence of God then we contemporary people need to be taught a way to do this. That is why we say Centering Prayer is not only a relationship but also a discipline.

Centering Prayer is also a discipline because it assists us in letting go of what I consider three of the major obstacles to the spiritual journey after we have kept the commandments and are living a responsible life. These three obstacles are overconceptualization, hyperactivity, and overdependence on self. *Overconceptualization* is always trying to figure things out. Don't get me wrong: there is nothing wrong when wanting to get a grasp on the things of life by analyzing them and trying to put them into some reasonable framework. This is part of our way of approaching life. Here I am speaking of overconceptualization. The compulsive and obsessive reasoning that never wants to let a thought go, that never even wants to try to let a thought go. We have experienced times in our lives when the thoughts "wag" us. There is something we have on our minds, that no matter what time of the day it is, it is right "in our face." We can't think of anything else. We are attached to our thoughts; we believe in Descartes' statement, "I think, therefore I am." Thinking becomes the centerpiece of our lives. Now I would like to suggest, if we are unable to let thoughts go at times, how is God going to put another thought in our minds? How is God going to give us some new information?

Hyperactivity: We find it hard to just sit doing nothing. We have to be always on the go. Yes, we have responsibilities that need to be taken care of. Yes, there are times when we are the only ones who can do it. But is this true all the time? I don't think so. After a while our activities run our lives rather than the opposite. At times I find myself a bit overwhelmed by my schedule. I guess I feel this especially when I am not feeling well. I have commented to the office staff about how busy the scheduling is. Then they remind me who is in charge of my schedule. Who else? I am the one; there is no one else to blame. How is God going to teach us some new activities—how can God make an appointment with us, so to speak—if we are all booked up? Apply this to your own situation. Where are the openings even in the routine of everyday life? Ours is a life of "doing" and not of "being."

Overdependence on self: There is a saying that "God only helps those who help themselves." That is not true, is it? God also helps those who do not help themselves. All too often we act as if everything depends on us. We have to be there for everyone, and if we do not take care of it ourselves it will never get done right. To a point this is true, but in another sense it is not. There is a friend of mine—I know he will not mind me telling this story— who has every conceivable communication gadget one could imagine. No matter where we go, if it is not the car phone, it is the cellular phone, if it is not the cellular phone it is the beeper. When we go to supper, it is a rare meal where he isn't called away to answer a beep, or ring, or vibration. Yes, a vibration. They now have beepers that don't beep but vibrate. What next? How can God get through to us if there is no space or even the realization that we are dependent on God?

I am not saying there is anything wrong with figuring things out in our lives. I am not saying that there is anything wrong with living a full life and being active. I am not saying there is anything wrong with depending on ourselves. But I am saying that we need to realize that there are times when we overconceptualize, are hyper about our activity, and depend too much on ourselves.

This is the way we have been raised; this is the tempo of the world. But we don't have to be stuck in that pattern of life. In fact if we are, then we are setting up some major roadblocks on our spiritual journey.

Yes, Centering Prayer is a relationship—a communion with God. Yes, Centering Prayer is a discipline—an aid to our dying to self, a dying that takes place by our letting go of overconceptualizing, hyperactivity, and overdependence on self at certain periods of time each day. The heart and soul of Centering Prayer is the consenting to God's presence and action in our lives: in other words, a coming apart with the Lord and resting so that the Lord can minister to us.

So let me share this prayer with you, a prayer that has been part of my life since 1975. There are four simple guidelines developed by Thomas Keating and presented by Contemplative Outreach.

1. Choose a sacred word as the symbol of your intention to consent to God's presence and action within.

2. Sitting comfortably and with eyes closed, settle briefly and silently introduce the sacred word as the symbol of your consent to God's presence and action within.

3. When you become aware of thoughts,* return ever so gently to the sacred word.

4. At the end of the prayer period, remain in silence with eyes closed for a couple of minutes.

Let me remind you again what Thomas Keating says about Centering Prayer:

> *Centering Prayer* is an effort to renew the teaching of the Christian tradition on contemplative prayer. It is an attempt to present that tradition in an up-to-date form and to put a certain order and method into it. Like the word *contemplation,* the term Centering Prayer has come to have a variety of meanings. For the sake of clarity it seems best to reserve the term Centering Prayer for the specific method of preparing for the gift of contemplation and to return to the traditional term *contemplative prayer* when describing its development under the more direct inspiration of the Spirit. . . . Contemplative prayer is a process of interior transformation, a conversation initiated by God and leading, if we consent, to divine union.

Let's look at some of the points which Fr. Keating makes. The first is that Centering Prayer is *not* contemplative prayer. We have said that Centering Prayer can be put into the category of receptive acquired contemplation, but it is not infused contemplation. The second is the desire to present Centering Prayer as an up-to-date form to prepare us for the gift of contemplative prayer, if the Spirit wishes to grant this gift. The third point is that if transformation is taking place within us, it is not Centering Prayer that is doing it, but the gift of contemplative prayer. The fourth is that Centering Prayer is a container for our consent and it is our gift of consent that attracts the Spirit to do what needs to be done. I will say more about this later.

---

*The term *thoughts* refers to any perception at all, including sense perceptions, feelings, images, memories, reflections, and commentaries.

Also, let me state that Centering Prayer is not part of *lectio divina* and *lectio divina* is not part of Centering Prayer. They are two distinct prayer practices. They do support one another, but they are not the same, nor should they be combined together when practiced. They can be done at the same prayer session but must be separated. The ideal would be for the Centering Prayer period to take place before the *lectio divina* practice. As I see it, Centering Prayer, besides being a communion with God, helps to prepare us to hear the Word of God on a much deeper level. By letting go of the thinking, the activity, the need to do everything ourselves, there is a preparation to be more open. The *lectio divina* session reminds us with whom we have a relationship—God through Jesus. This is not only a relationship of friendship but also one of responsibility. As we see what is expected we once again enter Centering Prayer to allow God's presence and action to do what needs to be done so that we can live up to our call. Centering Prayer and *lectio divina* are at one another's service; they dance together as they listen to the music of the Spirit.

The guidelines are important—I like to see them as a recipe for prayer. Getting the recipe straight is important to serve the spiritual food for which it was designed. What is that spiritual food—preparing for the gift of contemplation, if the Holy Spirit wishes to grant it? The gift of contemplation is truly a gift. All we can do is prepare for it. The same with the guidelines for Centering Prayer—they have been designed in order for us to be able to offer our intention to consent to God's presence and action within, while we let go of everything else except this intention.

When I was child, my parents owned a four-family house. Each week my mother would make the spaghetti sauce. The aroma would fill not only our apartment but the whole house. There was a young couple living on the first floor. When the husband came home from work and walked into the hallway leading to his apartment, he would be met by this aroma. He hoped that it would be coming from his apartment. Not so—his wife was not into cooking. He begged her to go talk to my mother about getting the recipe. Finally she did. My mother explained about the olive oil, sautéing the onions and garlic, adding the tomatoes and then the tomato paste at the right time, the proper seasoning and the three to four hours of slow cooking. How excited the young wife was to get the recipe and she said she would try it the next day. She did and the following day came to my mother, sad faced and disappointed. It did not work out. My mother was shocked at this and asked her to review the recipe to see what could have gone wrong. Yes, she had gotten the olive oil, sautéed the onions, and added some garlic, the proper seasoning, and the three to four hours of slow cooking. Well, what about the tomatoes and the tomato paste, my mother asked. "Oh, Mrs. Arico, they were so expensive I decided tomatoes are tomatoes and so I used ketchup instead." End of story. Don't fool around with the basic element of the recipe. The guidelines are also very important and need to be followed.

Let me now go through each one of the guidelines with you. *The first guideline:* Choose a sacred word as the symbol of your intention to consent to God's presence and action within. We choose a sacred word. Let's not get hung up with the term "sacred word"—we call it sacred because of its intent. When we pray the word it is a symbol of our intention to consent to God's presence and action within. That is what makes it sacred. It celebrates our consent. The example I like is how the Blessed Virgin Mary responded to the angel at the Annunciation, "Be it done unto me according to your word." The saying of "Yes, I do," to the Lord. Do whatever needs to be done for me to become what you want me to be. The "sacred word" is a symbol of this "I do."

There are many ways of choosing the sacred word. For our purposes here, I ask you to spend a few moments in prayer asking the Holy Spirit to help you in your choice. Next, I ask you this question: What name do you call your God when you have an intimate conversation with Him in prayer? When you are having a heart-to-heart conversation with God, what is your favorite name for Him? For example is it Father, Mother, Abba, God, Yahweh, Jesus, Christ, Lord, Brother, Savior, Spirit, Lover, Shalom? There are many names that God can be called, but what is your special name for Him? If it is not one of the above, do you have another? Pause a moment and chose one name, and one name only, a single word.

Now having done this, three things may have happened: one name came to mind immediately, many names may have come to mind and you had a hard time choosing one, or no name came to mind because you do not have heart-to-heart conversations with God calling God by name. Whatever the situation, please choose one name as your sacred word: a symbol of your intention to consent to God's presence and action within. Whatever sacred word you have chosen, please do not change it during the course of the prayer time.

The second guideline: Sitting comfortably and with eyes closed, settle briefly and silently introduce the sacred word as the symbol of your consent to God's presence and action within. Sitting comfortably means for the most part with your back straight and upright. Comfort during prayer is important because we are offering our bodies to the Lord; they are the temples of the Holy Spirit. We honor that by preparing our bodies for our time of prayer. We close our eyes to let go of visual contact with the world around us, pause a moment, and then begin to pray our sacred word. The praying of the word is very gentle like a feather being placed on absorbent cotton or like dew on a blade of grass. The praying of the word is gently repeated when needed to celebrate our intention, our "I do" to the Lord in the spirit of Jesus praying to His Father.

The third guideline: When you become aware of thoughts, return ever so gently to the sacred word. Notice carefully that phrase, "when you become aware." If there are times when you are not aware of anything because you are in the silence, then there is no reason to pray the sacred word. The term *thoughts* is an umbrella term for any perception at all, including sense, feelings, images, memories, reflections, and commentaries. Thoughts as understood in this context are inevitable, integral, and a normal part of Centering Prayer. When you become aware of them then return ever so gently to the sacred word. This requires a minimum of effort; it is the only activity we initiate during the time of Centering Prayer.

Let me give you some examples: When you are entering into the prayer and you begin to worry about things, then ever so gently return to your sacred word. You begin to get some new insights on how to resolve a problem: ever so gently return to the sacred word. You begin to be attracted to the ordinary sounds around you: ever so gently return to your sacred word. You begin to feel a little itch: ever so gently return to your sacred word. If it does not go away, scratch it. You begin to say to yourself, this is the silliest thing that I have ever done: ever so gently return to your sacred word. You begin to think that this is the most wonderful thing that you have done: ever so gently return to your sacred word. You begin to think of people you should be praying for: ever so gently return to the sacred word. You begin to picture Jesus walking down the street calling you by name: ever so gently return to the sacred word. You begin to remember good things that have happened in your life: ever so gently return to the sacred word. You begin to remember things that are not too pleasant that happened in your life: ever so gently return to the sacred word. You let them come; you let them go. Don't push them away. Don't try not to think about them. Just let them come and let them go.

This third guideline is a very important one—it is the basis for letting go and also dying to oneself. People have asked what happens if the thought is very important. I assure you, you will remember it when the prayer is over. Do you think that God only mentions things to you once? How many times has God had to repeat things to you, over and over again until finally you got it? If it is important it will be there for you after the prayer session.

I was told a story a number of years ago about a man who was beginning to do Centering Prayer, but he was also into recording his dreams. He had the habit that whenever he had a dream, he would write it down in his special book in the middle of the night, immediately after it happened. Then he started to do Centering Prayer. Now, I am sure you know that God has a sense of humor with those he loves. Well, let's call this man Mark. Mark started the prayer and in the middle of it he had a great insight on how to feed the poor of the world. From force of habit he wrote it down without thinking about it and continued with his prayer. Well, when the prayer was over he realized that he had written something about feeding the poor of the world. What he had written was "Xerox donuts." That's right: "Xerox donuts." He never again looked for a message in the prayer. Thanks, Lord, for your wonderful sense of humor with those who you know really love you.

The fourth guideline: At the end of the prayer period, remain in silence with eyes closed for a couple of minutes. Why do this? So that the reservoir of silence that has built up in you can be carried into the activities of the day. Silence is a powerful healer and sustainer. It helps give us a peaceful center so that when we return to the busy routine we can find ourselves responding to the events of our lives, rather than just reacting to them. I've heard it put this way—"It gives you a seven-second pause (as they have on the radio talk shows) to decide what you really want to do as the 'stuff' of the day begins to surface."

The recommended suggested time to pray the prayer is twenty minutes. It comes from the monastic routine that sets aside either fifteen or twenty minutes for various spiritual exercises. However, for your first-time experience now, I would recommend that you set you alarm—hopefully it has a gentle ring—for seven minutes. Try doing it now, following the guidlines on p. 127–28.

I invite you to let the Lord know that you really want to consent to God's presence and action within. Pause for a moment.

I invite you to call to mind your "sacred word"—the name you call your God in prayer, a single word. You have chosen this word as a symbol of your intention to consent to God's presence and action within. Pause.

You have stated your intention to the Lord, you have chosen your sacred word as a symbol of your intention to consent, I now invite you to pray this prayer or one similar to it.

> Father, Son, and Spirit; Creator, Redeemer, and Sanctifier, alive at the center of my being, I wish to surrender in love to you. May my sacred word—the name that I call you—which I will pray whenever I become aware of anything else, be a sign and symbol of my intention to consent to your presence and action within. Here I am Lord, here I am. Be it done unto me according to your word. So let me begin by ever so gently praying my sacred word only when I become aware of something else. So now I begin.

Set your timer for seven minutes. At the end of the seven minutes, pray a short prayer of gratitude, or if you wish, the Our

Father. I invite you now to close your eyes, settle briefly, and
begin to introduce your sacred word only when you become
aware of thoughts, feelings, sounds, or images.

Thank you for taking the time to pray the prayer. All too
often people will just continue to read rather than enter into the
experience.

Whenever I present this method in a workshop, which as I
said before is the best way to learn the prayer, I find that in the
question and sharing session after the first experience the reactions
fall into three categories. The first and most common is that so
many of the participants are amazed at how many thoughts they
had. It did not seem as if they had that many thoughts until they
entered into the prayer. Then the thoughts came like a hail storm.
They started very gently returning to the sacred word, but after a
while they were repeating it so many times it seemed to fill up the
whole seven minutes. The second group found themselves questioning the fact that this was prayer: it was so different. "This can't
be prayer. I know what prayer is suppose to be like. I should be
saying something besides that sacred word." So they begin to put
in special intentions, to pray for everyone who asked for their
prayers, and so on. The third group could not get over how fast the
time went by: they really felt that they were resting.

To the first group, I would say that thoughts are a normal part
of Centering Prayer: they will always be there, you cannot get rid
of them, you are not asked to empty your mind or stop thinking.
In this prayer there are no distractions unless you decide to get up
and leave or begin to think about the thoughts. In this prayer you
simply let the thoughts come, let them go, and don't react to them.
You don't retain them, you don't resist them—you simply let them
come and let them go. In spiritual terms this is called detachment
or holy indifference. You know they are there but you simply let
them pass. Like barges going down the Mississippi river heading
for the next lock, you just let them float on by.

To the second group, I would say that prayer is not only
words. In your other prayer periods you will have plenty of time
to pray for all your special intentions and that is important. At this
time, we simply communicate with our presence, with empty

hands, so to speak, realizing that the highest from of communi-cation is presence. Have you ever had a conversation with your loved one and had the sense that although he or she was sitting there right in front of you he or she was not really there? You might even find yourself saying, "Is anyone home in there?" Do not underestimate the power of your presence in prayer.

The third group rested in God's presence and entered into that rest. Sometimes it is described as being asleep and this caus-es the person some concern. I always say so what, what makes you think you are more pleasing to God awake? I like to tell the story about one of my nieces. I would go to her home and she would come and sit with me—she was four years old at the time —and we would talk. She would end up telling me everything that her mother told her not to say. After a while she would fall asleep in my arms. Did she love me less? I don't think so. I even must admit that I felt closer to her as she slept in my arms than when she was talking. It was a funny phenomenon that when she would awak-en she would pick up her conversation right where she had left off. Prayer is not our performing for God; it is our being with our God. Sometimes we do fall asleep and it could be just what we needed at that time. Most of the time we were just resting in God's presence; it seemed as if we were sleeping.

The important thing for all three groups to remember was that we were *praying*. We had the intention to consent to God's presence and action within. We did not take back that intention. We were praying. In fact I always like to comment when I have led a group in Centering Prayer that no matter what was going on in each of us, we were together raising up a glorious hymn of consent to God. What greater gift can we offer?

Just some additional comments before I invite you to pray the prayer for twenty minutes.

It helps to have what we call a vestibule in preparation for the prayer—pick a good time, a comfortable place, read a short Scripture to remind you that you are entering into a relationship with God and that you are joining thousands of others who are drawn each day to this prayer throughout the world.

Pick a timer that has a gentle alarm.

Remember this is a prayer of intention not attention. You are not being asked to be attentive to anything that goes on in the prayer. The heart and soul of Centering Prayer is your intention to consent.

Sometimes the sacred word will get vague in the sense that you don't even realize you are praying it—this will happen at times after a while.

The sacred word is not said with your lips or with any sound; it is prayed internally.

It is recommended that you pray the prayer twice a day for twenty minutes each—once in the morning and once later in the day.

One of the most frequent objections that I receive is that people do not want to say yes to God so completely. We are not sure we want to consent to God's presence and action within us. We don't know what God will have up the divine sleeve if we say "yes." We are not sure if we trust God that much to give Him a blank check. I have found that the big issue with people who are open to the spiritual journey is not one of faith or charity; the issue is trust.

There are a number of comments that I make. The first is to say, "Are you having such a great time of it now that it could not get better?" As if everything were perfect now. Most people will begin to smile when they hear that comment because there is always room for improvement.

The second is, "Have you not consented to others?" What do I mean? Well, let me give you an example. Have you ever gone into the hospital for an operation. OK, think about what happened. You went into the admissions office and gave them all the vital information. You signed papers that said no one was liable, not the doctor, the surgeon, the staff—this is costing tens of thousands of dollars and no one is liable. They then put you in a wheelchair and place you in a room you did not choose, with a roommate you would never have chosen. The nurse comes in to give you some pills. You ask what are they for, and the nurse gives you a look and says, "You know I have had a very hard day I don't need you giving me trouble—takes these pills or I will have to get the hospital psychologist to talk to you." At a time you least expect, a nurse comes in to prep you, in parts you don't even look at or touch. Then two people come to put you on a cart and wheel you to the operating room, talking about everything and everyone but you. You are wheeled into an operating room that is cold, are met by seven people with masks on, knowing only that one of them is the surgeon. You will find out the other names when you get the bills. They are playing music to soothe the surgeon (no one asked you what music you would like to hear). The anesthesiologist asks you how you are doing and before you can answer the mask is on and you are in a deep sleep. Now, after watching *ER* and *Chicago Hope,* I am not too happy about what goes on between the surgeons while we are cut wide open. I don't think we need that negative energy. Then they wheel you back to your room. You have pains they never told you about and they discharge you within twenty-four hours because they say you will receive better care at home. Now why did you go through all of this? Because everything you could do for yourself did not work. The pills did not work, the exercise did not work, the diet did not work, the alternative medicine did not work, the healing prayer service did not seem to work. You finally had to surrender to another to work on you on levels you could not get to by yourself. Why? Because you wanted to live a better quality of life. You wanted to be more of what you were called to be in body, mind and spirit by the Lord. You knew you could not do it yourself, so you said "yes" to another. You said "yes" to the healing presence of the qualified people on the hospital staff. A friend said to me after reading this that it was too negative. Of course it paints an extreme situation. My point is that if we can so trust others, as in this case, why can't we trust God?

And so it is with God. All the resolutions, pilgrimages, and novenas did not seem to get you what you needed and so you surrendered in prayer to allow the Divine Physician to do what had to be done on levels in your spiritual being that you could not get to by yourself. Are you still anxious about consenting? I hope not.

I invite you to pray the prayer for twenty minutes.

Let me review the four guidlines again.

1. Choose a sacred word as the symbol of your intention to consent to God's presence and action within.

2. Sitting comfortably and with eyes closed, settle briefly and silently introduce the sacred word as the symbol of your consent to God's presence and action within.

3. When you become aware of thoughts, return ever so gently to the sacred word (see page 128).

4. At the end of the prayer period, remain in silence with eyes closed for a couple of minutes.

Once more, I invite you to let the Lord know that you really want to consent to God's presence and action within. Pause for a few moments.

I invite you to call to mind you sacred word—the name you call your God in prayer, a single word—you have chosen this word as a symbol of your intention to consent to God's presence and action within. Pause.

You have stated your intention to the Lord, and you have chosen your "sacred word" as a symbol of your intention to consent, I now invite you to pray this prayer or one similar to it:

> Father, Son, and Spirit; Creator, Redeemer, and Sanctifier, alive at the center of my being, I wish to surrender in love to you. May my sacred word—the name that I call you, which I will pray whenever I become aware of anything else—be a sign and symbol of my intention to consent to your presence and action within. Here I am Lord, here I am. Be it done unto me according to your word. So let us begin by ever so gently, praying our sacred word only when we become aware of something else.

Start you timer, which is now set for twenty minutes. At the end of the twenty minutes, pray a short prayer of gratitude or, if you wish, the Our Father.

Once again, thank you for taking the time to pray the prayer.

If you have additional questions refer to the leaflet in the appendix on *The Method Of Centering Prayer.* Most of the questions are answered in that leaflet.

Please also remember that Centering Prayer does not take the place of your other prayers; they are still important and essential for you. Centering Prayer just completes the picture of what prayer is all about.

7 ❈

The Cloud of Unknowing *and Contemplation*

I have a copy of the late fourteenth-century classic, *The Cloud of Unknowing*, author unknown, edited by William Johnston, which I have read so many times that it has tape around it to keep it from falling apart. I don't want to part with it: it is a good friend. I am sure you have experienced this with some of your favorite books.

The Cloud speaks strongly to the Centering Prayer practice and, like the material in chapter 2 here, grounds the practice in the Christian contemplative tradition. Basil Pennington has summarized the major themes of *The Cloud* as follows:

- If one strives to fix one's love on God while forgetting all else, which is the work of contemplation, the goodness of God will bring one to a deep experience of God.

- Even Christians called primarily to a life of active service must at times lay aside their activity and give time to meditation and communion with God.

- One must be a person of faith, sufficient faith to believe in the Divine Presence hidden beyond the cloud of unknowing.

- One must have turned from sin toward God in love, a love strong enough to make one seek God in the darkness of God's incomprehensibility, leaving behind other attractions and desires.

- It is not what you are nor what you have been that God's all-merciful eyes see, but what you desire to be.

- It is God, and God alone, who can fully satisfy the hunger and longing of our spirit which, transformed by God's redeeming grace, is enabled to embrace God by love.

I find this an excellent overview which gives the background for the following themes that I would like to develop: the use of the simple word and detachment, the loss of self, the place of Christ, and the primacy of love. For a more complete presentation I refer you to William Johnston's introduction.

Use of the Simple Word and Detachment

The author of *The Cloud* suggests that during prayer all thoughts, all concepts, all images must be buried beneath a "cloud of forgetting" by the use of a simple word:

> If you want to gather all your desire into one simple word that the mind can retain, choose a short word rather than a long one, a one syllable word such as God or love is best. Choose one that is meaningful to you, then fix it in your mind so that it will remain there, come what may. This word will be your defense in conflict and in peace. Use it to beat upon the cloud of darkness about you. Subdue all distractions, consigning them to a cloud of forgetting beneath you.

> It is best when this word is wholly interior without a definite thought or actual sound.

So when you pray the word, you don't think about the word and you don't think about how the word sounds. You just be present with the word.

The author makes a distinction between finding God in the "cloud of unknowing" and putting everything else into the "cloud of forgetting." Elsewhere he says:

> You are to concern yourself with no creature, whether material or spiritual or with their situations or doings, whether good or ill. To put it briefly, during this work you must abandon them all beneath the cloud of forgetting.

This is truly the spirit of detachment which is called for on the contemplative spiritual journey; it is not easy, but it is not impossible with God's help:

> Should some thought go on annoying you, demanding to know what you are doing, answer this with one word alone. If your mind begins to intellectualize over the meaning or connotation of this word, remind yourself that its value lies in its simplicity. Do this and I assure you these thoughts will vanish.

Why? Because you have refused to develop them, you have accepted that they will be there and then just let them go.

These are wonderful insights that will stand us in good stead with regard to Centering Prayer. As the third guideline of Centering Prayer states, "Whenever you become aware of a thought, ever so gently return to the sacred word." The insight here is the gentleness, the single word and the importance of being detached. Let me share an example: If I decide to have a conversation with one person in a room, I am letting go of every one else in the room. I will simply not be attentive toward them. I do not demand that the others leave. That would not be polite because they are part of my life. I simply carry on my conversation. That's what the sacred word does. It focuses our intention on one thing and lets everything else pass by, or sets other things aside for the time being.

The Cloud of Unknowing never explains the method of prayer in detail. Method was always taught from teacher to student. The ramifications of the method were always written. Today everyone looks forward to seeing the "how to" spelled out in detail. When you teach something new in a book, you do take a lot for granted. There is not the opportunity for questions. Let me use an example. Every time you get a cookbook, the author of the cookbook presumes you know how to use the stove. If, of course, you don't know how to turn the stove on, the cookbook is rather unimportant. You never can be sure where the reader is. That was the thinking behind the practice of not writing out the method in those days. Each person comes to a book with a certain mindset. The author cannot anticipate all the questions and all the mindsets. That is why the best way is to learn the method in a workshop or a personal presentation.

The Loss of Self or a Sense of Separation from God.

The notion of the loss of self can be described in a variety of ways:

> Now we come to the difference between the contemplative work and its counterfeits, such as daydreaming and fantasizing. These originate in a curious or romantic mind, whereas the blind stirring of love springs from a sincere and humble heart.

The author is trying to answer people who say "you're just dreaming." The intention is the key item. If the intention is flowing from a curious mind, or an overly romantic idea of what resting in God is all about, then the end result will by a counterfeit, not really contemplation. But if the intention flows from a sincere and humble heart's stirring of love for God, then this is authentic. We simply want to be in the presence of God. We are not curious to get any message, or any ideas or concepts.

Now he shows the importance of being in touch with our feelings:

> He alone understands the deep universal reason for sorrow who experiences that he is. Every other motive pales beside this one. He alone feels authentic sorrow who realizes not only what he is but that he is. Anyone who has not felt this should really weep for he has never experienced real sorrow.

When we experience ourselves as we are, we become aware of our creaturehood. We are not all that we should be in the eyes of God. This self-awareness is the coming to grips with our impression that we are separate from God. Most of our depression and loneliness and anger comes from our feeling that God has walked out on us. That's only an impression. God is never separate from us. But we do have a powerful collective and individual illusion that God is separate. When we experience this separateness, often called dryness, and when we interpret the dryness and sorrows and trials as God's absence, then we experience these normal emotions with exquisite intensity.

The feeling is like that of being an orphan. We feel alone in a rather hostile universe. And we want someone to take care of us. Part of our journey is recognizing that inside us is this little twinge. "My heart will not rest until it rests in You." We know there is a journey, but we don't always recognize that it is a journey to nowhere. We think we have to go somewhere and be someone different than who we are. When we think that, we feel the separateness most acutely.

The loss of self can be understood best as the dying of the false self. When we experience both a hunger for completeness and the feeling of separateness, we are on the journey. The loss of self never causes a loss of identity. We become who we are called to be. .

The Place of Christ

The third component is the place of Christ. We can never lose sight of Christ on this journey. An example from *The Cloud* is helpful here (p. 17, chap. 17). In the Martha and Mary story, "Mary turned to Jesus with all the love of her heart, unmoved by what she saw or heard spoken about her." Mary ignored the noise and bustle of Martha. We might say Mary was a "teflon listener," letting Martha's bustling slide right past her. She couldn't control Martha, but she was able to let her sister's comments go and prevent them from distracting her as she sat at the feet of Christ.

> She sat there in perfect stillness with her heart's secret, the joyous love intent upon that cloud of unknowing between her and her God . . . for as I have said before [*Cloud,* p. 18] there never has been and never will be a creature so pure and so deeply immersed in the loving contemplation of God who does not approach Him in this life through that lofty marvelous cloud of unknowing.

She lets everything go. "It was in this very cloud that Mary directed the hidden yearning of her loving heart." She was with the Lord and let everything else go.

It's important not to lose sight of Christ on our journey. People have entered into the contemplative journey and felt Christ was calling them to the Godhead, beyond names, beyond terms. They assume they can bypass Christ, forget the names Father, Son, and Holy Spirit and venture out into the oceanic experience of Godhead. We need a way to venture out and to get back. It is Christ who is causing this movement. Christ is our way, the truth, the light, the life, our pattern. We must never forget that it is Jesus who is our guide and companion on this journey—he has the map:

> Anyone who aspires to contemplation must cultivate study, reflection, and prayer.

The author is concerned about our being grounded. *Lectio divina* provides us with the framework for this journey. We don't just "surrender" and float into a contemplative state and stay there. The cyclic rhythm of *lectio divina* helps us to remain grounded. Jesus is our guide and the Scriptures keep us grounded on this journey. They provide the guidance of the Holy Spirit, the necessary wisdom for the process of discernment about what is happening in our lives. We need all the help we can get to come to fuller understanding and fuller responsibility.

The Primacy of Love

The last dimension is the primacy of love. The author of *The Cloud* says:

> This is what you do. Lift up your heart to the Lord with a gentle stirring of love, desiring God for God's own sake, and not for God's gifts.

This is the purity of intention that is needed in order to pray with pure faith:

> For in real charity, one loves God for Himself alone above every created thing. One loves fellow human beings because it is God's love.

In the contemplative world, God is loved above every creature, purely and simply for Himself. The heart of this work is a naked intent toward God for the sake of God:

> Thoughts cannot comprehend God. Though we cannot know Him, we certainly can love Him. Beat upon the thick cloud of unknowing with the dart of your loving desire and do not cease, come what may.

So when we move into the prayer, it is pure love. People who love don't have a list of things to do. Just spending time with the one we love takes center stage of our attention. Early in the relationship, there is much to "do," but as the relationship matures the doing becomes secondary to the loving part of the relationship.

Married folks tell it this way: After the day's work of running, working, doing, and sharing, we are sitting next to each other enjoying each other's company. That's not the time to start reminding each other of the crack in the ceiling that needs attention. It is the time to be with one another. That also applies to God. We don't always need to remind God of all we need. The Father knows what we need before we ask. Trust Him. There is plenty of time to bring to God's attention the list of things which need to be done during the other prayer periods. Now is the time simply to be with the Lord.

What kind of love are we talking about here? The author of *The Cloud* continues:

> So to stand firmly and avoid pitfalls, keep to the path you are on. Let your longing relentlessly beat upon the cloud of unknowing that lies between you and your God.

You cannot apprehend or conquer God through knowledge. But you can through love:

> Pierce that cloud with the keen shaft of your love. Spurn the thought of anything less than God and don't give up this work for anything.

For the contemplative, the work of love by itself will eventually heal.

This is the heart of the matter. Contemplative prayer removes the roots of sin and begins a deeper healing process. We can spend our whole lives on the surface, dealing with symptoms. It's the difference between pulling a weed out by the roots and merely mowing the lawn. Even that analogy is weak because it is not our effort that removes the roots, it is the Divine Gardener.

When we enter with our intention to love and trust, we move into the presence of God in the cloud of unknowing and at the same time we are inwardly healed over and over again.

What Contemplation Is Not

I am always surprised but not amazed at how difficult it is to grasp what contemplation is. In my reading I have made a list of what various authors say that contemplation is *not*. I would like now to share this with you.

First, contemplation is not a relaxation exercise. We may find ourselves relaxed in doing it, but that's a side effect.

Contemplation is not a charismatic gift. Charismatic gifts are not given primarily for the good of the person but the good of the community. One charismatic gift that might help open us to the gift of contemplation is the gift of tongues. In this gift we have the ability to communicate with God in words we don't understand. So we give up the need to understand: our praise is beyond the words we usually use and know.

Contemplation is not a mystical phenomeno. We are not talking about bodily ecstasies, visions, words spoken in imagination or impressed upon our spirit. In fact, most spiritual writers advise us to let those things go if we get them. They could interfere with the journey because there is always the danger of focusing too much attention on them. They're more trouble than they're worth. We may begin to rely more on the mystical phenomena than on God.

Contemplation is not a para-psychological phenomenon, such as the knowledge of things at a distance, control over bodily functions like heartbeat and breathing, levitation, and out-of-body experiences.

Contemplation is not a "spiritual high." We may not feel anything in particular, either high or low.

Contemplation is not blocking out all of reality in order to remain empty. Some people expect this, but we are not supposed to make ourselves empty. We're supposed to be detached. The Spirit will do whatever needs to be done in opening us to the grace that is needed so that we may be able to let go.

Contemplation is not a rare reward for excellence or virtue. This has nothing to do with our achievement or status. It's a gift. It can come to anyone.

Contemplation is not a singular mark of God's special love or approval so that we can enter into the contemplative dimension. It is an ordinary development in the life of a faithful, praying person.

Contemplation is not a luxury option in our spiritual life, it is part and parcel of the journey.

Contemplation is not a merge into a void. This is to allay the fears of those who have a smattering of knowledge about Eastern forms of meditation and believe that if we meditate too long we will lose our identity.

Contemplation is not a dissolving of our personality like a drop of water into the sea of God's being. We don't get absorbed and lose our personality.

Contemplation is not detaching our soul from our body so that we might have an altered state of consciousness.

Contemplation is not higher consciousness.

Contemplation is not the absence of pain or the absence of desire.

Contemplation is not self-knowledge.

Contemplation is not a state of God-like goodness.

Well, then, what is contemplation? Father Thomas Keating puts it simply and authoritatively: "Contemplative prayer is a process of interior transformation. A conversation initiated by God, and leading, if we consent, to divine union."

So then what is Centering Prayer? "Centering Prayer is a method designed to facilitate the development of contemplative prayer by preparing our faculties to cooperate with this gift."

8 ❈

Passive Purification: True Self, False Self

There is an ancient tradition called the Senses of Scripture which refers to the various levels of meaning in the Scriptures; they are usually four in number. The first and the last are the literal level and the unitive level. The two in the middle have various labels, but for my purpose I will call the second level the moral and the third the allegorical level. Each captures a particular sense and depth of meaning in the reading of the Scriptures. The literal speaks in terms of really listening and understanding the text. The moral talks about the application of the text to daily life—the living of a good moral life. The allegorical moves into the dynamic of the text in the sense that readers begin to see new implications in the text that make them rethink and re-experience not only the text but their lives. The unitive refers to becoming the word that is read. The words of Scripture become so much part of them that they change their lives. I bring these facts to your attention because I have taken them and applied them to the spiritual journey and the purification that takes place when we consent to God's presence and action in our lives. Let me make the application.

The first is the *literal level*. On our journey it is important that we have the facts, the knowledge of what this is all about.

It means that there needs to be a belief system, sacramental rituals, an awareness of the importance of the commandments, and a need for personal prayer and public worship. On this level, we are concerned about the data, the commentaries, and the details that go into the understanding of the basics. Knowledge is important, but it is not enough; there needs to be an application of that knowledge. I heard a story about a Catholic university where the highest mark in theology was earned by a non-Christian student. He had the knowledge but had no intention of using it other than as an academic tool. On the other hand, I know Christians who attended all the required programs in religious education in their youth and have no desire as an adult to learn anything more about our faith. There is always something new to learn about our faith, our religious beliefs, and the spiritual journey. We must be open to this new knowledge.

The second is the *moral level*. This is the application of all we have learned on the literal level. We find ourselves moved by the Spirit to apply the insights and lessons to our lives. We decide to do some things a little differently. We make resolutions. Many good people stop here. Being a morally good person is the end of the road for them. They have arrived. They are doing their duty and doing it quite well. They are truly responsible. It is said that one of the ways to frustrate the working of the Holy Spirit in life is to "stay as a morally good person." There is more to the journey. The events of our lives and the prompting of the Holy Spirit tries to make that clear to us.

The third is the *allegorical level*. Here we have to deal with the presence of Christ in our lives. He acts like the two-edged sword spoken about in Scripture. He is alternately consoling, confronting, and purifying us. We begin to really look at our lives: to see them through the eyes of Christ, not just through our own eyes. We begin to discover the seamy side of our selves. We see our "shadow," as C. G. Jung calls it, the repressed side we don't let anybody, especially ourselves, see. We see our deeper faults and hard-heartedness, as well as our tendency toward self-ishness which displays itself in so many ways.

I have heard it described as a viewing of our inner geography, showing us our deepest distorted selves as well as our gifts gone awry. When we see our faults and selfish tendencies, we see how hooked we are to certain patterns of behavior.

The sword also cuts the other way. It gives us the opportunity to be able to see the gifts that God has given us, the talents that we have, the good that we have accomplished, the people we have touched. Sometimes we are so dominated by a false sense of humility that we do not allow ourselves to see how good our God has been to us. I believe that it is at this level that we really see what needs to be healed, what needs to be forgiven, and what needs to be celebrated. We must not forget these three aspects. They help us focus on the whole picture.

At this point, we are in touch with the fourth, *unitive level*. We become purified and as we do, our true selves emerge more in everything we do. Merton observes that "You don't discover God until you also discover the real you." When we reach the unitive level, we allow ourselves to be embraced by God. A oneness takes place so that we can say with St. Paul, "I live now not I, but God lives in me." We are truly living our heritage—living in the image and likeness of God.

Our spiritual journey has various levels to it. In the process of being touched at these various levels we are becoming the "new creation" that St. Paul speaks about. We must consent to allow the Spirit to move us along these various levels, doing the work which each demands.

Let us explore some of the elements that are involved in this process: passive purification, the true self and the false self, and active purification.

Passive Purification

It is important to remember that when we consent to the divine presence and action in our lives in prayer, especially in Centering Prayer, we are preparing for the gift of contemplation, if the Spirit grants it. Passive purification is one of the fruits of the gift of contemplation.

In a world where hectic piety is the norm, we have to shift gears to appreciate passive purification. It doesn't sound like virtue to our ears. The word passive is especially suspect. After all, passive is what we are in front of the television set. How can that be a way to arrive at unity with anything, much less God?

The apophatic tradition understands that while we are passive, God is not. God is the active agent. Our being passive is a way of acknowledging that we are creatures and need to be receptive. What our Creator does is more important. We can't make the sun come up, or the rain fall and, if the spiritual truth be known, we're not very effective at rebuilding our inner life either.

Concerning passive purification let me share several quotes from Thomas Merton's classic, *New Seeds of Contemplation:*

> Contemplation does not simply "find" a clear idea of God and confine Him within the limits of that idea, and hold Him there as a prisoner to whom it can always return. On the contrary, contemplation is carried away by Him into His own realm, His own mystery, His own freedom. It is a pure and virginal knowledge, poor in concepts, poorer still in reasoning, but able, by its very poverty and purity to follow the Word "wherever He may go."

The gift of contemplation brings us into God's territory, so to speak, on God's terms, beyond our ordinary way of seeing and hearing what is involved in the spiritual journey. In another passage from this same source Merton says:

> Let no one hope to find in contemplation an escape from conflict, from anguish or from doubt. On the contrary, the deep inexpressible certitude of the contemplative experience awakens a tragic anguish and opens many questions in the depths of the heart like wounds that cannot stop bleeding.

Many times people are attracted to Centering Prayer with the hope of peace and rest—this is not the purpose. The heart and soul of Centering Prayer is consenting to God's presence and action within. In that consent and opening ourselves to God, God allows us to face the worst and the best in each one of us. When we consent to God on those terms then it means that God will take full advantage of this most generous offer. Ed Farrell, a priest and writer from Detroit, often said, "Be careful of what you ask for, God may give it to you." He especially made this comment with regard to Charles de Foucauld's Prayer of Abandonment, which captures the spirit of passive purification.

> Father
> I abandon myself into your hands;
> do with me what you will.
> Whatever you may do, I thank you:
> I am ready for all, I accept all.
> Let only your will be done in me,
> and in all your creatures—
> I wish no more than this, O Lord.
>
> Into your hands I commend my soul;
> I offer it to you with all the love of my heart,
> for I love you Lord,
> and so need to give myself,
> to surrender myself into your hands,
> without reserve,
> and with boundless confidence,
> for you are my Father.

The prayer reads, "I abandon myself into your hands. Do with me what you will." At that point we are moving from the moral into the allegorical level of the journey. We are saying to the Lord, "Please take over and do what needs to be done." Let me add a personal note here. I have prayed this prayer for over thirty years and I have added my own phrase to the prayer. Just before I pray that final line, "for you are my Father," I say "and I consent to your divine presence and action in my life." I verbalize in the prayer the intention which is the heart and soul of Centering Prayer.

My father died of cancer in May 1987. He went quickly, thank God, only three months after being told he had cancer. During that time he fell in love with this prayer. He kept it right next to him at all times. He asked that it be on his memorial card. The copy of the prayer which I gave him came from the Little Sisters of Jesus in Rome. On the back of the prayer was a picture of Charles de Foucald. At the time of my dad's death we all commented on how he looked just like the picture of the man he came to love. He used to say to me, "This is my buddy."

True Self

Let us continue with Merton's description of the process of purification as it applies to the true self; he calls it "the inner self":

> The inner self, as secret as God, and like God, it evades every concept that tries to seize hold of it with full possession.

This is a rule of relationship. Try to possess a friend and see how quickly you lose your friend:

> It is a life that cannot be held, studied as an object, because it is not "a thing." It is not reached or coaxed forth from hiding by any process under the sun, including meditation. All we do with any spiritual discipline is produce within ourselves something of the silence, the humility, the detachment, the purity of heart, the indifference which are required if the inner self is to make some shy, unpredictable manifestation of His presence.

What is this true self we are talking about? Merton again:

> The secret of my identity is hidden in the love and mercy of God. . . . Therefore there is only one problem of which all my existence, my peace and my happiness depends—to discover myself in discovering God. If I find him, I will find myself and if I find my true self, I will find him.

So the true self, "is hidden in the love and mercy of God. . . . If I find Him, I will find myself and if I find my true self, I will find Him."

Thomas Keating in *Open Mind, Open Heart* says this about the true self:

> Our basic core of goodness is our true self. Its center of gravity is God. The acceptance of our basic goodness is a quantum leap in the spiritual journey. God and our true self are not separate. Though we are not God, God and our true self are the same thing.

Any journeys into self-knowledge are journeys into finding God. From my point of view the journey into self-knowledge is made up of four parts.

The first part is my need for self-knowledge. I discover God in learning about myself. If I try to discover God without knowing myself, I discover a God outside myself. There is no God only outside myself because God is everywhere.

After learning more about myself, the next step is accepting myself. If I can't accept myself as I am, and as God exists within me as I am, I am stuck. As Keating has said, "The acceptance of our basic goodness is a quantum leap in the spiritual journey." This is a difficult part of the process. We carry so much baggage. The records playing within concerning the lack of affirmation as we were growing up, demand affirmation now. I tell people that the great gift which they give themselves when they go into therapy is not only "self-knowledge" but more importantly "self-acceptance." Jesus put it well: "Love your neighbor as you love yourself." Love flows out of self-acceptance. We need help in accepting the truth about ourselves. It is a necessary step.

The third step is self-opening. That means I want to be open to the spirit working in me to lead me where I need to go. This is another example of a crossroads situation. I know my self and I accept myself—therefore I have it together. On one level "yes" and on another level "no." On the level of human growth, well done. On the level of spiritual development—I need to move on. I cannot stay put. That is, I need to be open to the Spirit and deal with the false and the true self that I have accepted. I must consent with my whole being to the presence and action of God in the process or I will stagnate.

The final step is self-surrender. Having consented then to self-knowledge and self-acceptance and opened ourselves to the working of the Spirit, then we must surrender on a deeper level to the Lord. We must carry through on what we are now aware of; in a sense, go with the flow.

Although all four parts are important in this process, the pivotal one is self-acceptance. Dealing with ourselves is not an easy task. We are our worst enemies at times. Let me give some examples. We know how we get upset when other people misjudge us, we know we need to take some steps and be more open to the Spirit at work in our lives. But if we haven't accepted ourselves and the fact that we're getting upset when people misjudge us—if we haven't learned to acknowledge that—we will invariably short-circuit this process. The true self is found in this self-acceptance. The false self can hide by refusing to accept what is known. It is in this tension that the Holy Spirit is at work. Can I accept myself in all my frailties? That's where I find God. Knowing my weaker, less attractive components is one thing, accepting them is another. Can I accept my gifts? That's where I also find God. Knowing my strengths, my attractive and gifted side is one thing; accepting them is another.

Let me share a story. I had just finished giving a weekend retreat followed up by a training program for presenters of Contemplative Outreach in Florida—ten days of intense but fruitful work. Both were well received and the comments were fabulous. Many of the participants came up to me and shared personally how much they appreciated my work and presence. One of the staff whom I worked with during these days said, "Do you hear what they are saying?" I answered, "Well, yes, I hear them." I answered in a way that really was saying I did not hear. She continued, "God is giving you a gift; these people are telling you how good a job you did and you are not hearing it. But I know if there were some criticism you would hear it right to the core of your being." Yes, she was right. I did not hear it. I heard it but did not take it in. I did not allow myself to celebrate the gift God was giving me. I did not hear the praise, but I know I would have heard and taken in a critical comment. This is an acceptance issue, isn't it? We need to accept it all when we open ourselves to the Spirit, then we are able to offer all of it.

False Self

Merton goes on to speak of the false self:

This is the man I want myself to be but who cannot exist because God does not know anything about him. And to be unknown to God is altogether too much privacy. My false and private self is the one who wants to exist outside the reach of God's will and God's love—outside of the reality and outside of life. Such a self cannot help but be an illusion. We are not good at recognizing illusions, least of all the ones we cherish about ourselves—the ones we are born with and which feed the roots of our sin. For most people in the world, there is no greater subjective reality than this false self of theirs, which cannot exist. A life devoted to the cult of this shadow is what is called the life of sin.

"My false and private self is the one who wants to exist outside the reach of God's will and God's love—outside of reality and outside of life." These are powerful words. False self is the self we create in our own illusions. We think it exists, but it really doesn't. There are within us centers of knowledge, honor, power and love that help us choose the false self over and over. But what we are called to do is to reverse the journey by returning to God and find ourselves in him. We must go back by the way we came. The path lies through the center of our own soul. We must withdraw ourselves from the attachment to exterior created things and our interior illusions about ourselves to find God. Thomas Keating has this to say about the false self:

> The false self develops in opposition to the true Self. Its center of gravity is itself. . . . Our basic core of goodness is dynamic and tends to grow of itself. This growth is hindered by the illusions and emotional hang-ups of the false self, by the negative influences coming from our cultural conditioning and personal sin.

We must regain possession of our true selves by liberation from anxiety, fear, and inordinate desire of our false selves. In practical terms we are talking about a practice whereby what is alive in our unconscious begins to surface in order that we might be free of it. In *Open Mind, Open Heart,* Keating comments on the process, but when he is speaking about contemplative prayer here he is really speaking about Centering Prayer:

> When the unloading of the unconscious begins in earnest, many people will feel they are going backwards, contemplative prayer is just impossible for them because all they experience when they start to pray is an unending flow of distractions. Actually, there are no distractions in contemplative prayer, unless you really want to be distracted or if you get up and leave. Hence, it doesn't matter how many thoughts you have. Their number and nature have no effect whatever on the genuineness of your prayer. If your prayer is on the level of thinking, thoughts would be extraneous to your reflection and would be distracting. But contemplative prayer is not on level of thinking. It is consenting with your will to God's presence in pure faith. Emotionally charged thoughts are the chief way the unconscious has of expelling chunks of emotional junk. In this way, without your perceiving it, a great many emotional

conflicts hidden in your unconscious and affecting your decisions more than you realize are being resolved. As a consequence, over a period of time, you will feel a greater sense of well being and inner freedom. The very thoughts you may lament while in prayer, are freeing the psyche from the damage that has accumulated in your nervous system over a lifetime.

In Centering Prayer, both thoughts and silence have an important role to play. The thoughts carry what needs to be healed and the silence creates the space for the healing to take place. This is what the tradition understands as the passive purification of the false self. The false self is being healed as we open and surrender ourselves to the Holy Spirit applying the gift of contemplation. Centering Prayer sets the stage for this to happen, but by itself it does not have this power. It is the contemplative gift that does the work—in other words the Holy Spirit.

Let us look at the story of Lazarus coming out of the tomb. Jesus tells Martha He wants to do something about His friend's death and asks where he has been taken. Martha warns Him about her brother, "He's going to stink! He has been in there for four days." Apparently, Jesus doesn't mind the smell. He calls Lazarus forth from the tomb and says something very important: "Untie him." We do not know how difficult it was for the "untie" command to be carried out or how painful it was for Lazarus. We are all bound up in one way or another. We are all in knots in certain areas of our lives. How often we use the phrase, "My stomach is in a knot." Untying is what passive purification is all about. When we are all tied up, we can't free ourselves, regardless of all our squirming. Our own effort is futile; we need someone else's help. We cannot do it on our own.

What needs to be untied? What are we faced with? Within us are emotional programs that were planted in us as we were growing up. They are active. The emotional programs are what one might call the "ill advised teachings" of parents, teachers, church leaders, community, media, peers—the list is long. We have records playing in us that others have placed there. We have a veritable old-fashioned juke box inside of us. We're playing everybody else's songs but our own. We may not even know yet what our songs are. Press certain buttons and we get a prerecorded message. Who is this talking? My parents? Or teacher? Or coach? Or, heaven forbid, a television commercial? Does the true self want to say what I just said? Or worse, does it want to feel what I'm feeling? Messages like "Never put anything in writing." "All men are a dime a dozen." "Those types of people are inferior (or superior) to me." A common horrible one: "Break any commandment except the sixth and ninth." These prerecorded records are subtle, affecting our judgments, emotional responses, and world view.

We are deeply affected by our cultural conditioning. For example, we unconsciously live our lives out of a Western model of religious attitudes rather than a gospel model.

The Western model says that we initiate all things and God rewards. We assume that God rewards the same way our culture does. Success is earned, money is earned, so heaven must be earned, too: "Everybody knows that." What is worse is that we all "know" it, so we reinforce each other. And we know it on such a deep level, it is difficult to eradicate. After all, it's our cultural identity, like speaking English and believing in democracy.

In the West, external acts are more important than internal ones. For example, you don't get a raise for internal intention. So you can expect the corollary: look good. Look good even if what is in your heart has nothing to do with you looking good. This applies to our religious attitude.

The Western religious model emphasizes future reward and punishment. If you do good, good will be returned to you and the opposite is also true. For example, I am living my life now for a reward in heaven, which is a terrible shame. Don't get me wrong: I am not against going to heaven, but usually when we adopt that future reward position, we miss the fact that we are being rewarded right now by God.

The gospel model predates our industrial mechanical revolution and consciousness. The gospel model's admonitions are not amplified by our cultural dispositions, so they are harder for us to hear or follow. Let's listen to some of them. The gospel values tell us that God takes the initiative. We receive and are called to respond. It is a misunderstanding to say that it is better to give than to receive. We have received more than we have ever given. In our culture we don't know how to receive well. We have received everything, beginning with our DNA inheritance. We have been receiving all our lives. The new ecological consciousness is underscoring that on a cosmic level. When we take for granted all that we have received, then we lose sight of God's presence in us and in the world around us. God always takes the first step.

In a gospel frame of reference, internal acts are more important than external ones. It is where our hearts are that counts. How we look in the eyes of others is secondary, or not really important. We can be divided against ourselves when our values are not reflected in our actions. The word "divided" is the correct word here. It creates stress and tension for us. There is a sense that the soul is being split—divided between the call of the false self and the call of the true self within. St. Paul talks about times that he felt as if there were two people inside of him: The things I want to do I do not do, the things I don't want to do I do.

The emphasis in the gospel is on the love of God and neighbor now—not tomorrow. Now is the time to show the love. For example, where am I coming from when I say I will love and forgive if you shape up? The loving should always be there, even if it is manifested in "tough love." A sharp dichotomy exists between the values of the gospel and western culture. For example, when we listen to the gospel, who can really buy into loving our enemies? The Western model insists that if someone hurts you, you hurt him back—with interest. We take revenge and then ask for pardon. The usual understanding of the phrase "to turn the other cheek" is simply not acceptable in our culture and time. So we have a Western juke box inside us, playing interesting material that interferes radically with any gospel values.

Energy Centers

When we are born we are quite needy little creatures. We demand that these needs be taken care of. Let's call them instinctual needs which are naturally part of any human being. They are the need for survival, the need for affection, and the need for control. Let's look at them. When we were born there was a need for security and survival which was furnished by our caregivers, by our parents when they fed us, clothed us, and gave us a safe space to live, which we came to know as home. This is true for most of us; there are of course exceptions. We also had a need for affection and esteem which was determined by the loving we received, how our self worth was celebrated, and how much we felt a part of our family. As we were growing up we wanted to be the center of everything in the beginning, but with time we learned that we had to be "part" of the family and not the center of the family. We could not be controlling everyone. This is when we learned that there were limits and restrictions. We hear phrases such as "No," "Do this," "Learn to play nice," "Do that one more time and I will have to punish you." All these instinctual needs were very important for the growing-up process. Now here is the situation. If these needs were not met by our parents and caretakers, or if we perceive they were not met, then as we grew up we created a whole system of compensatory needs and programs which I am calling "energy centers." These energy centers are at the root of the way we act and react habitually and spontaneously to the people and the events of everyday life. So there is a major need to always be in control, or to make sure we are secure or getting all the credit we deserve.

When our buttons get pushed, not only does a tune start playing on our juke box, but also a marching band strikes up. We mobilize lots of information and energy in the service of these responses which are fed by the energy centers of power and control, affection and esteem, security and survival. Here we are talking about a disproportionate response to a situation because these compensatory needs are not being taken care of or met. For example, the inability to just let go is a control issue at this time and then becomes a lifetime issue with a particular person or group. Here we have some brothers and sisters who got along fairly well when they were growing up, but there were two of them who were never quite comfortable with one another. Later there is a problem with a sick parent: one is asked to do most of the caring and begins to feel resentment toward the others—so much so that they haven't talked with one another for years. Was it the parents' fault or was it something deep-seated from childhood? Who knows for sure? What we do know is that no one is talking, which is quite a disproportionate response to a normal family situation. Something got stuck, somewhere.

Any pattern of disproportionate responding cannot only be rooted in created compensatory needs, but can also be rooted in how we are programmed for success. When we were growing up what was the message we may have received from our parents? "Whatever you do, make sure you are a success. Make sure you do better than we did." Was this not the message that many of us received as we were growing up? Do better than our parents, which means be more successful? Now there are certain rules and regulations that go into being successful. Make sure you are always in control of what is going on: don't let anyone take advantage of you and make sure you get everything that is coming to you. In other words have the power, be in control. Make sure you are well thought of by the important people. Remember it is who you know that counts. Above all make sure you never make a mistake. If you do make a mistake make sure you get out of it and save face. You must never fail. Oh, it was not put exactly that way, but it was implied.

Whose values are these? Gospel? Or Western culture? It seems to me that a person who never makes a mistake, is always well thought of, and always in control isn't on much of a spiritual journey. If it is a journey it is one which has been self-imposed. It is not the journey we are called to by Christ. If we look at Christ in the Gospels, it seems that Jesus was looked upon as having made a mistake. He was not well thought of and was out of control, especially during His passion and death. He certainly was not well thought of by the important people. If you think He was in full control, go back and read His prayer in the garden. I ask you to consider these questions. How can Jesus get through to a person who always has to be in control? How can Jesus teach someone who will never admit he has made a mistake? How can Jesus teach a person to really love when she is only interested in impressing important people? Once again, please do not get me wrong. It is OK to be well liked and well connected. It is OK to be a person who has a handle on life. It is OK to try to work so hard that you do not make mistakes. The problem is in the degree of attachment—the term I have been using is to be "disproportionately attached," or to respond disproportionately to the lack of these things pertaining to power, affection, and security.

On our spiritual journey we can get all upset when we do something wrong, or say something offensive. It bothers us when things are happening that we can't control, when people do not think well of us, or we are made to feel uneasy. We feel like we are falling apart. Unless this is part of an abusive situation, we should be thanking God for these times. This may be exactly what needs to happen at this time of our lives. Often it is not the true self that is falling apart; it's the ill-advised teachings of the culture that makes up our false self that are unraveling like Lazarus's bandages. The Lord may be untying us and it does not feel good at first.

Our responses are so unconscious that they are hard to recognize. These records seem to play without our permission: they are so much a part of us. The way they slowly get erased is when we enter into a regular routine of prayer—especially Centering Prayer. Well, that's not entirely correct: we don't do the work in Centering Prayer, God works on us. As we consent to God's presence and action within (Centering Prayer acts as a container for our consent), the Spirit works on us to dismantle the false self material we have inherited or acquired. This is the power of prayer, for on our own we are not aware of what we should do or even ask for without the help of the Holy Spirit.

I'm not saying we can't desire survival and security, control, or the esteem of others. When these desires are a preference, that's fine. When these needs are becoming an addiction—when these needs are so crucial we will do whatever is necessary to obtain them, no matter what the cost—then they are deleterious. We need to have them *or else*. Then they interfere with our spiritual journey. When we feel these preferences are owed us by life, then it is an addiction. It happens subtly. It is so subtle we can't attack it openly, that's why deleting and dismantling these inordinate desires is the gift of passive purification. It can only take place when we surrender and allow the Spirit to do it for us.

If we try to get rid of these addictions by an active frontal attack, we will inadvertently use the same thought processes and assumptions we are trying to get rid of. If we have to be in control of getting rid of our control needs, we are creating more control needs. If we have to be secure in getting rid of our security needs, we are creating more security needs. If we have to be building our esteem as we get rid of our esteem needs, we are creating more esteem needs. One begins to create a circle of activity that is self-defeating and the present state of our soul is worse then before. There was a religious community that took great pride in its humility. Careful, this part of the spiritual journey can get quite subtle.

If you think you don't have a false self, just call in four of your best friends and discuss your tiny little faults and moods.

What we also tend to need to let go of is our overidentification with our peers. I am not saying that we cannot be proud of our group and of the teachings we have received from parents, school, church and country. What I am saying is that this over-identification can be an obstacle for us on our journey. We need to take a look at the people around us and see if they are in line with gospel values. We are never too old to change and let them go. To live is to change, and what we change are the false teachings we've made our own—our own false selves.

Passive purification does not debilitate our natural powers. The natural power that we have in each center is not made weak. It is made clear. Healthy preferences for order, security, and pleasure are always a gift from God. What is not from God is our clinging addiction to these powers so that if we don't get all the attention we need, we become distraught, difficult, and belligerent.

We know that these attachments are getting the best of us when we begin to have feelings that we don't care about anything and we can't shake those feelings. Other times we feel sad and grieving with a sense of loss or we begin to feel unusually angry for little or no external reason. Some of us at times become acutely aware of sensual desire, and we have a difficult time with feelings and sensations of lust. Sometimes we even get a strange feeling that we are perfect and everyone else seems inferior. When we have these strange visitations, the solution is not to get busy, smile with denial, and be happy or spend more time with our pets. If we use these band-aid solutions, we are, in effect, just mowing the lawn, not pulling anything out by the roots.

Let me tell you a story. When I was on sabbatical at the Vatican II Institute in Menlo Park California in 1987, we had the custom each evening for one of the thirty-three priests in the three-month-long program to preside at the liturgy and to preach. One evening a priest from Iowa was presiding. At the homily time he shared this story:

> Every summer I spend time on my family's farm to help with the plowing. [He then proceeded to walk up and down in front of the thirty-two of us, acting out the tractor going back and forth across the field. He added the sound effects also.] Putt, Putt, Putt, Putt, Putt, Putt, Putt, Putt, [I am sure you can imagine what we were thinking as the thirty-two of us watched him going back and forth.] Bang, the tractor came to a stop. It hit something in the middle of a field that my family had been plowing for over a hundred years. I got off the tractor to take a look. There was a large rock in the middle of the field. I tried to move it but I could not. To make a long story short it turned out to be a half-ton boulder that was in the middle of the field. [He then paused and looked at each one of us before he spoke again.] That, my brothers, is what the spiritual journey is all about. When you keep yourself open in prayer and open to the working of the Holy Spirit in your life, you never know what will come up, but whatever does come up must be let go of because the Lord is making more space for the divine farmer to plant the new seeds deep.

What a powerful story. If things are happening in our lives, they are happening because we are leaving ourselves open to the work of God on levels deeper than we can get to on our own. So then the feelings and reactions that we become aware of are opportunities of saying yes to our God. It is God showing us what needs to be dealt with in our lives for healing, forgiveness, or celebration.

This is what passive purification is all about during our prayer time and in the activities of each day—the Spirit making us look at many things including the energy centers in our lives and how they control us more than we realize. So when we start questioning ourselves, then the work of the Spirit is stirring within us. What are some of the questions? Listen: "Who is in control of my life that I did not give permission?" "Who is not applauding in the manner I expected?" "Who knows something about me because I allowed myself to be vulnerable?" "Has someone discovered I am not perfect?" The energy centers create all the static, all the unprofitable turmoil. These three centers amplify every longing, every fear, every need until they capture our attention fully.

We don't look at the energy centers within us because our emotional programming says everything is normal. We buy into this agitation. We become more determined to meet all the neurotic needs of those three centers: we will get fully in control, we will get all the recognition we deserve, and we will gratify every sensate whim—or so we think.

Let's start with the premise that we are going to make some more mistakes before we die. Thank God! If we determine we are going to be always secure and right, how can we grow?

For a second premise, let's assume not everyone is going to like us. So what else is new? Not even Jesus was able to get everyone to like Him and what did He do wrong? Isn't it a relief to know that we can at times be unrealistic in our expectations?

Let's also start with the premise that we think we are always in control. So when we don't get our way, what do we do? Is our way always good for us?

There are different ways we act out when our needs are not fulfilled in the area of control, esteem, and security. It is interesting when we look at the political dynamic. I am sure we remember how in a past presidential election, one of the themes influencing the people was, "It is the economy; that is the issue." Here I believe it all comes down to "It is a control issue." We don't want to appear out of control before others and even with our God. We want to be in charge. Here I believe it also comes down to "It is an esteem issue." We don't want to be thought less of by others and by God. We want to be well regarded. Here I believe it also comes down to "It is a security issue." We don't want to feel uneasy or unsure before others and our God. We want to be sure of ourselves. When we cannot be in control, or feel secure or experience esteem, how do we respond?

One approach is *withdrawal*. We say, in effect, "I'm going to take my toys and go home. I'm not going to play in this community any more." "I'm not going to talk to my family any more." "I'll be darned if I volunteer to cook any more. No one likes my cooking anyway." Does this sound familiar?

Another approach is to be *aggressive*. No one can approach us because all our artillery is bristling. "Just cross me once and I'll blow you out of the water." We may say we never do things like that. We are not that aggressive. OK, then how about being passive-aggressive, withholding our interest and becoming cold as ice at the appropriate time? The aggression is there in one form or other. Many people doing really good work, especially social action can at times come from a position of aggression. That's why Merton says we need to sit and meditate and make sure our reform desires are coming from the right place in our heart. Reform can legitimize our anger and aggression. Look at the turmoil in countries where there is dissatisfaction with the leadership. Very rarely is the movement for reform nonviolent, and when there is violence it is justified, rationalized, and glorified as being necessary. Many times the new leaders fall into the same pattern as the old leadership and the circle of violence continues.

Another approach is to become very *dependent*. We want our needs to be taken care of by another. We fawn on whomever is in authority. We want to be well-connected. If authorities forget to say hello or forget the slightest social deference, we are back in our room wondering why that authority (boss, bishop, superior, coach) doesn't like us. We are still looking for "good boy" and "good girl" strokes. That's a block. We need to be respected and valued, but if the slightest slight from authority causes us inner chaos, it wreaks havoc on our lives.

Then there is the most subtle of approaches, let's call it *capitulation*. We give in, we go along with whatever is happening for the sake of peace hopeful that eventually we will get our way. In other words, we work a deal.

All these responses or approaches—withdrawal, aggression, dependency, and capitulation—are temporary solutions. They do not get to the heart of the matter: the letting go of our over-dependence for happiness and success based on power, esteem, and security. When we disproportionately hold on to them, then we create monumental blocks on the journey to transformation. Notice the word that I use again: "disproportionately."

So what can we do? Let me present this in two ways. When we talk about purification, we can look at it as passive and active. The passive is consenting to God's presence and action in our lives. By our fidelity to prayer, for example—a real praying of our prayers, allowing the spirit to work more deeply in us by the practice of *lectio divina* and Centering Prayer—we are granting permission for the Divine Physician to do what needs to be done. We are open, we are receptive and our prayer practice sends that message: Do what you need to do, Lord. The example of the plowing story is a good one about allowing whatever needs to surface, to surface. The passive not only gets to the roots, but it also prepares the way for our active approach.

Active Purification

Active purification is the concrete approach of facing our problems and dealing with them using all the resources at our disposal. Now that we are aware of what underlies what is going on in our lives, we need to face up to it. As an example, now that the field has been plowed and prepared, it is time to do our part to plant the seeds of new life.

So what can we do? Whenever we are aware of a situation, which we feel caught up in, unable to think clearly, or are losing sleep over, look at what is happening and then pray for guidance from the Holy Spirit. Ask the Spirit to give us the eyes to see and the ears to hear what is happening.

First, label the situation. Identify the feeling and identify the energy center that seems to be affected: sometimes all three of them are. Call it for what it is. In the labeling there is a freedom. Don't justify it; don't make excuses for it. Label it. We hate being out of control. We are sad when we are not well thought of. Label it. We are disappointed when people don't think we're perfect. Label it. It doesn't work to just try to let it go. Taste it. Walk through it. We need to see that false self within that is messing up the present moment because we're buying into it unconsciously. We shouldn't get angry at ourselves: we didn't know our record was playing so loud.

Having taken this first step, I invite you to say a prayer. The prayer is simply one word, "Welcome." Say it as often as you like. What are you welcoming? You are welcoming this special gift that God is bringing to your attention for healing, forgiveness, or celebration. If you really believe that God works in, through, and with the events of your life, then you believe God is present in this situation. So "welcome" that presence. You may not feel like welcoming the event itself, but welcome God's presence in the event.

Then apply what I like to call the antibiotic with a statement such as this. "I let go of my desire to control this situation— Welcome." But wait, you may want to control this situation in the long run, which is all right, but at this moment and time you seem to be out of control, so you offer this to God—inviting God to take control. But rather than say it in so many words, "Lord, I desire control, I always desire control, but this is out of control. I raise up my inability to control the situation to you; do what you need to do to control it as you will"—just get to the heart of the matter instead and say: "I let go of my desire to control this situation—Welcome."

Will this solve the problem? No, not at that moment, but it helps you let go for a few moments of the static and disruption around the event. You make some room for the Lord to come and do what needs to be done. It leaves an opening to help you respond to a situation rather than react in your usual way, which many times makes it worse.

Attitudes for the Journey

As we deal with this question of purification, true self, and false self, there are some things which we should keep in mind. I like to call them "attitudes for the journey."

First, we need to welcome and befriend our dark side. It is part of us—our own dark side. It is not a stranger, it is part of what we bring to prayer and to all of life. The alternative is denial. We have a choice, either denial or the truth. As usual, the truth sets us free. The energy of the dark side, when it is freed up, is going to be part of what we need for transformation. Self-knowledge and self-acceptance as we have said is essential. We have to show compassion to ourselves. I think it is also permissible to laugh or at least chuckle at our dark self. Maybe Dante had a point when he called his epic about the spiritual journey *The Divine Comedy*.

When we deal with our dark side, we begin to see that many people or events that annoy us are really gifts. They are the ones who activate our juke box, so they bring our dark side out in the open where we can acknowledge and deal with it. Then these records in our juke box can begin to be erased by the Spirit through prayer. Part of our contemplative journey is identifying and owning these problems. (I am talking here about the normal situation, as much as anything can be normal. I do not apply this formula to an abusive situation, where definite measures need to be taken and it is more than just a matter of letting go. But sometimes the letting go can give even these persons the opening to have the courage to know they are not trapped in a certain situation. In this opening they can come up with a plan of action to free themselves with the help of God. Many times when there is no such opening, a person feels there is no other way to live or survive than in this abuse.)

The second attitude to develop is to keep in mind that God is totally on our side, despite any evidence to the contrary. It is God's good pleasure to facilitate our personal growth and integration. It is for this we were created. When children are struggling and not doing very well, a loving parent will do everything he or she can do to help, seeing the child's desire to get it right. The parent will take the deepest pleasure at seeing the child's growth and integration. We call God our parent because we believe that this is God's attitude toward each of us. We have some records playing in us that do not see God as loving; rather they present God as distant and disapproving. Those records need to be disposed of or altered.

The third attitude is to realize that our need for healing draws on the infinite mercy and compassion of God. Isn't it amazing that as we get older and further along on the journey we are more willing to see our faults, to see what needs to be healed? We say things like, "I have an unbelievable amount of rage which I cover up by smiling. That rage shows itself again and again, and I need healing." It's so wonderful to admit that kind of thing. Then we confront the realization that it is entirely possible to be in a rage and still love God. We have the passion; we need only to redirect it. God has been watching this going on for years, waiting for the moment when we show a willingness to bring it to Him. As we grow older, we get more in touch with the mercy of God. We always knew God's mercy was there, but on the other hand we were not quite sure. Now we can really receive it.

The fourth attitude to remember is that trust leads to perfect love. If we trust, trust happens. Fear is useless. The fear usually is mostly in our head and has little to do with the reality of the situation. As the trust grows, so does the love. Most of the time on our spiritual journey we are looking at our own stuff. These are things that need to be healed and forgiven. Now we get to a point where we hear the Lord say, "Enough already—when are you going to look at me?" Life is more than our own concerns and worries. It is also relating to God. Bishop Fulton Sheen, the famous Catholic television personality of the '50s used to say, "Look up and live."

Thomas Keating has this to say:

> The growing awareness of our true Self, along with the deep sense of spiritual peace and joy which flows from this experience, balances the psychic pain of the disintegrating and dying of the false self. As the motivating power of the false self diminishes, our true Self builds the "new self" with the motivating force of divine love.
>
> The building of our new self is bound to be marked by innumerable mistakes and sometimes by sin. Such failures, however serious, are insignificant compared to the inviolable goodness of our true Self. We should ask God's pardon, seek forgiveness from those we may have offended, and then act with renewed confidence and energy as if nothing had happened.

Let me leave you with this closing thought: God is calling us out of our tombs. How do we come out of our tomb? Well, God is unwrapping us already in the passive purification process. Our tradition says that when we surrender to God in silence, we begin to heal. For our part, we can actively identify the material that surfaces outside of prayer time and look at these three centers of control, esteem, and security. Please don't reduce this to psychology—this identification is more than that. In the absence of faith, much of this is futile. The proper use of these three centers can be found in the reading of the first three Beatitudes. A contemplative is simply a person who lives the Beatitudes. We tend to skip over the Beatitudes—they don't seem practical to our culturally conditioned mind. It would be well worth our time to do the *lectio divina* prayer with the Beatitudes. They are the "wisdom" teachings of Christ.

9 ✣

The Fruits of Centering Prayer

What are the fruits of Centering Prayer? Notice I said the "fruits" and not the "effects." There is no cause and effect approach to the fruits of Centering Prayer. The heart and soul of Centering Prayer is "consent"—consent to the presence and action of God in our lives. There is no particular effect that we are looking for, no particular fruits that are desired as a primary focus. The prayer is simply an "I do," a consent, as pure and simple as anything can be in this life. And yet the willingness to say, "I do" to a commitment with the Lord is quite profound. It is in the spirit of Blessed Virgin Mary's *fiat*. Any fruits that come will come as a result of the power of consenting. Centering Prayer is a container holding our intention to consent.

Let me once again present the distinction between Centering Prayer, contemplative prayer, and contemplation—it is important that it is seen that the fruits are not necessarily flowing from Centering Prayer in itself but because Centering Prayer opens us for the gift of contemplative prayer. It is the gift of contemplative prayer which produces any fruits that we may experience. The fruits are not necessarily experienced during the time of prayer but in the events of everyday life through the working of the Holy Spirit.

As Thomas Keating puts it:

Centering Prayer is an effort to renew the teaching of the Christian tradition on contemplative prayer. It is an attempt to present that tradition in an up-to-date form and to put a certain order and method into it. Like the word *contemplation,* the term Centering Prayer has come to have a variety of meanings. For the sake of clarity it seems best to reserve the term Centering Prayer for the specific method of preparing for the gift of contemplation and to return to the traditional term *contemplative prayer* when describing its development under the more direct inspiration of the Spirit. . . . *Contemplative prayer* is a process of interior transformation, a conversation initiated by God and leading, if we consent, to divine union.

In our tradition this work of transformation is under the direction of the Holy Spirit. We now turn and look at the working of the Spirit within us. In Paul's Letter to the Galatians 5:22–26, we have a list of the "fruit of the Spirit": love, joy, peace, patience, kindness, goodness, faithfulness, humility, and self-control." Sometimes we don't pay much attention to what is listed, but the list is all about transformation. The first three are in relationship to God, the second three in relationship to others, and the final three in relationship to ourselves. In other words, these fruits put a face on the commandment to love God, neighbor, and self. Notice Paul does not say "fruits" the plural, but "fruit" the singular. They are many aspects of the one Lord. When we are baptized we are given the potential seeds of this fruit. When we allow the Spirit to work in us, these seeds are just waiting to be called and come forth from us.

There are two possible ways to allow the Spirit to work in us. Let me tell you a story about the renter, the landlord, and the house. It's the dead of winter. All the windows of the house are frosted. So the renter goes from window to window and scrapes off the frost. It's an endless task: as each window is cleaned and the renter starts working on the next one, the one he has just finished starts to frost up again. Then the landlord comes in and says, "You don't have to do that. All you have to do is make a fire in the fireplace and soon all the frost will disappear."

Unfortunately, our spiritual journey has been presented to us largely as a window-scraping endeavor. We weren't told about the fire inside, or we heard about it but did not really believe it.

It's not easy to say "yes" to the fire, but that is what we have to do. The fire is the Holy Spirit.

The "fruit of the spirit" is there to transform us, as Paul tells us in Ephesians 4:22–24:

> So get rid of your old self, which made you live as you used to—
> the old self which was being destroyed by its deceitful desires.
> Your hearts and minds must be made completely new. You must
> put on the new self which is being created in God's likeness.

What does "new self" mean? We are talking about a restructuring of consciousness which takes place, empowering us to perceive, relate, and respond with increasing sensitivity to the Divine Presence in, through, and beyond everything that exists. The "new self" comes forth as we deal with our false self. When this process is finished, we call it "the true self" as I explained in the previous chapter. We can't do that with resolutions: it's not just a few moral feats. The Spirit needs to be free to roam the corridors of our hearts and minds making us new. We need to give permission for the Spirit to roam wherever She wants to go. I have this image of the Spirit looking into every room in my soul, even those I would prefer not be looked into at this time. When we consent, we are giving the Spirit permission to do whatever needs to be done.

My mother lives in a beautiful one family home in New Jersey. She prides herself in keeping it "nice." Recently some major repairs had to be done. I called in a man who was recommended by the local church to look over the house. In a sense, he roamed the corridors from top to bottom and not only pointed out what had to be done, but with my mother's consent did it. If you looked closely at the process, there were these elements, an invitation, an appraisal, a plan agreed to, the carrying out of the plan, and the final payment for this particular job. Eventually nothing would have been done to the house, without my mother's consent. All changes and repairs in life come at a price. This applies to all of us: there are certain things we cannot handle on our own; we have to call the expert in to do the work.

Exterior Fruits—Those Seen by Others

What are some of the fruits I have seen in people's lives as a result of their taking time to enter into receptive acquired contemplation according to Centering Prayer, in order to receive the gift of infused contemplation? These fruits differ sharply from person to person, of course, but there are general ones that I have heard from people who are faithful in their prayer and begin to experience the gift of contemplation.

The first is an ability to let go. We have that little saying, "Let go, let God." Many times that is a band-aid statement. If we really mean "let go," we mean letting go of control, esteem, and security. This letting go can begin to take place in our lives by perhaps looking at "stuff" that we overidentified with, it could be as simple as what happens when we go shopping. Let's say we're pushing the grocery cart and we have seven items. We are in a hurry today. We go to the express lane of twelve items or less. We look at the cart in front of us and we actually count nineteen items! We cannot believe our eyes. Years of training and prayer go out the window as we begin to feel the rage rising. He's seven over the limit! We have a number of choices at this moment. We choose to utter in a stage voice, "Isn't it a shame some people can't count!" This is said out of a deep sense of justice, of course. I leave your imagination to work out the details of the rest of the story. Life is a series of such instances of letting go of little things, for the most part, before they get out of hand and become "big" things. Can we let the little things go? Did not the Lord say something about dealing with the small things in life preparing us for the bigger challenges? We never know how many spiritual battles are won in the supermarkets of our lives.

The second fruit is that we learn to receive, rather than always give. It is not easy to learn how to receive—we are better givers. To receive, to allow people to minister to us is a wonderful gift. To receive favors, to ask for help, to admit we are human, these are gifts of the Spirit. To invite someone to give to us so we can receive, we have to be ready for one of four answers: "Yes," "No," "Maybe," "Let me think about it." If we allow others freedom, the situation has nothing to do with whether they love us or not. We can manipulate people if we don't allow them to say to us: "Yes," "No," "Maybe," "Let me think about it." Learning how to receive is not that easy and yet we have been receiving from God and others all our lives.

We learn to love people on their terms, which is a matter of profound respect. We are responsible *to* each other but we are not responsible *for* each other. We can neither predict nor make another do what we think she or he should do. We do have to send out the best and clearest message possible. What a person wants to do with that is his or her choice. That doesn't mean we don't care. But we don't want to program people to be like tennis partners who hit us exactly the serve we want so that we can look good. I guess the test is how we handle the unexpected, not only in tennis but also in life in regard to our love of people.

Centering Prayer has an effect on our relationship with our other prayers and devotions. Because we make time for Centering Prayer, for a taste of silence, we find that our reading, meditation, and intercessory prayer begin to have a different energy. The One we are reading about, thinking about, and praying to comes alive for us in a new way. The relational aspect of prayer cuts through: it is no longer just saying the words. It not only affects our private prayer but impacts on our time at church and with our prayer groups. Because there are greater moments of interior silence in our lives, according to Centering Prayer, that silence nourishes and expands our appreciation of all our prayer and worship activity. We begin to hear the words and appreciate the sacred ritual on a deeper level. It is as if we are hearing and experiencing them once again for the first time. After all, the contemplative dimension is "the rest of the story" of our tradition.

People began to realize that much of everyday work was done out of compulsion and routine. The routine was so ingrained that it was done without attention or intention; it was just done. Now we realize how we "sleep-walked" through the day. Let me put it this way: we can do our work or carry out our responsibilities either from compulsion or compassion. When we see this, there is a chance for a change of approach and attitude. Let me give some examples. It dawns on us that when we are working out of compulsion, we insist that we are in charge of the project. We don't want to hear from anyone else. All suggestions need our clearance. And only we should be thanked at the end of the project. Everyone knows this was our baby. We did the work and we expect the recognition. We did a perfect job and we don't want to hear one word of criticism. That's compulsion.

The compassionate person can say, "Yes, I'm in charge, but if someone comes up with a creative idea or shows some initiative, I'll empower her to run with it. You don't have to check everything with me. And at the end, if my name is misspelled on the thank you notice, that's insignificant. It's also all right if some people disapprove or misunderstand. Think of all the good that was done for the others who experienced the program." You may say, well, that isn't the real world, but maybe it should be. Let me ask you this: What is the fruit of compulsion, what is the fruit of compassion in your experience? I will leave it up to you to give the answer.

Another fruit is the gradual transformation process (the journey to the true self by the letting go of the false self) which takes place in our lives. Let me tell a story about transformation. I was giving a retreat up in Hamilton, Canada. I was talking to about a hundred sisters in the chapel. There were forty sisters in the infirmary who listened to me over the speaker system. At the end of the retreat, the forty sisters in the infirmary wanted to meet me. I met twenty in a meeting room and then went to visit the others who were room-bound. The infirmary was the top of the line and each room was well appointed and immaculate. This is one of the pluses of the Canadian pension and health care system. I entered the room of an elderly nun who had had a stroke and couldn't talk. Our eyes met, she smiled, and I didn't want to leave. She didn't say a word, but I intuited a wonderful sweetness in her. That visit meant so much to me because two rooms away, I entered an identically appointed room where another sister was in the same condition. Our eyes met, but there was no smile, no nothing; I got what I will call "the look." I could not wait to get out! I could sense her anger, depression, and joylessness even though she spoke not a word. As I was leaving the infirmary, I spoke to the sister who was in charge and who was with me throughout my visit. I shared with her my impression concerning the two sisters. She was amazed that I had intuited so much in such a short time. The sister who was peaceful was a sister who had a hard life in community. Not in the sense of personal difficulties, but she was the one who was always sent to difficult assignments and did so willingly. The other sister, the angry one, was always a "big shot" in the community. When she got sick and was unable to continue her duties, she turned bitter and angry at God and everyone else. One sister had surrendered to God's will throughout her whole life, even in illness, and was transformed; the other one, who had been always in control, refused to give up her control when illness came and, it seemed became bitter and turned to vinegar. In a sense she was deformed. Why? I will leave the answer up to you.

In the transformed person a light comes from within that is not a product of one's personality or efforts. It is that manifestation of receptivity that allows the Spirit to work within. What is projected forth is a fruit of prayer. People can sense this presence, this other dimension. We can't program it. It happens. We have heard that saying, "Who you are speaks so loud I cannot hear what you are saying." Usually we hear it said in a negative context, but here I believe it manifests what I am saying: there is the Divine Presence within that colors all that is said and done.

Another fruit is a greater sensitivity for "the cries of the poor." I always found it interesting how everybody loved Thomas Merton when he wrote *New Seeds of Contemplation,* but people thought he was "going off his rocker" when he started talking about nuclear weapons, war and peace, poverty and racism. Everyone loved Henri Nouwen when he wrote *Wounded Healer,* but when he started to talk about Latin America and the handicapped in North America, he lost some of his followers. Fidelity to prayer moves the transformed person to really see the poor and no longer deny their existence. I think of Ferdie Mahfood, the founder of Food for the Poor. He tells his story of how Centering Prayer opened his eyes to the poor—opened them so wide that he could not see anything or anyone else but the poor. That yearning led to his establishing the organization that has given hundreds of millions of dollars worth of food and supplies to the poor in the Caribbean, especially in Haiti.

Entering into the contemplative way does not cause us to navel-gaze; it opens our eyes to more than we bargain for—we get the complete picture whether we want to see it or not.

Interior Fruits—Those Experienced Inwardly

In Centering Prayer, people begin to go from their thoughts about God to God. The third guideline of Centering Prayer says that whenever we become aware of any thoughts (commentaries, images, sense perceptions, memories, feelings), we should ever so gently return to the sacred word. This letting go in the prayer causes a ripple effect for letting go outside the prayer. This can pertain to many things, but here we are referring to God. They just go to God. Now, thoughts are needed for us to get to that point, but we have this intuitive impression that previously we were with our thoughts about God rather than with God. Of course this is just an impression that we had: we were actually always with God. It is like two people in love: after a while they stop thinking about the person they love; they just love the person. In a sense it is like looking at a picture of a loved one or being with the loved one. These are two distinct and profoundly different experiences.

Our false self begins to die. Those inner tendencies toward selfishness begin to lessen. The attitude that we must always be increasing in order to please God is gradually replaced by a decreasing of self. We realize that we are being carried. That is why the prayer "Footprints" is still so popular. There were two sets of footprints on the sand, yours and mine, God. And when there were problems in my life then there was just one set of footprints on the sand. Where were you, God? The answer: "Did you not know I was carrying you?" There is such a freedom to really believe that this is so—that God is always carrying us whether the times are good or difficult.

Because the false self is dying we develop a greater awareness of the presence of God in everything. It is not a "mind trick" where we keep saying "God is everywhere"—it is a genuine intuition that affects all we see and do. It is what is called, "praying without ceasing." It is not a case of just saying words but of being present to the presence of God. It is like diving into the ocean of God's presence all around us and within us. This is hard to put into words, but there is no doubt in our minds and hearts that this is so. I know that when I am on an intensive ten-day Centering Prayer retreat that I am very aware of how God's presence is in and around me. It is like having a new pair of eyes. It is like a new visual awareness. It is hard to explain, but it is there.

Some report a healing of deep hurts which have led to real human growth. I have seen this happen especially with the separated and divorced people who I ministered to when I was doing full-time family life ministry work in the '70s. I was asked to give retreats and workshops on Centering Prayer to these people. Many found great comfort in the prayer, especially the letting go aspect of it. They could consent to someone they could trust—their God. As I write this, I can recall their faces and remember their stories. It looked as if it were the end of everything for them; and then after that transition period there was a new life: the old saying about how "grace builds on nature." When healings take place, where the woundedness of a lifetime begins to heal, then we see some spectacular resurrection events: people who were thought to be dead have come back to life again. I could tell you many other stories of such healings, even within myself.

I have an image I want to share with you. Some have said this is a political statement. The exact words were, "That's a political approach—sure to please no one." I don't see it as a political statement, but rather an example using political terms. Let me take a chance that this will be understood in the way that I intend. I am talking here about an attitude and mindset that is part of each of us, depending on the circumstances. Within each of us is a Republican, a Democrat, and a mystic. God help us all. The Republican within us says, "I should be able to do it by myself. I have the ability and the strength. Only weak people need to depend on others." The Democrat part of us says, "If only some people would do something for us. If we only had a different environment, a different setting, a different partner. It could have been, should have been better." The mystic looks and says, "Yes, that is all true. But there is a much larger dynamic going on that we will never fully understand. This dynamic, God's plan, goes far beyond our plans and attitudes."

We need all three attitudes and mindsets on our journey. There needs to be an independent spirit within us: the grace to be able to stand up for what we believe, to live according to our conscience. I think of Thomas More's spirit of independence and courage as portrayed in the movie *A Man for all Seasons:* an independence that came from his willingness to face new challenges and stand up for what he believed.

There also needs to be in us a spirit of cooperation and dependence, to know we are part of the human family, that our gifts and talents need to be shared. We have to do for others and allow them to do for us when necessary. We are part of the "mystical body of Christ": we need one another.

Finally, there needs to be in us a spirit of the mystic, a realization that we are part of the larger picture beyond what we see, hear, taste, feel, and smell. Merton speaks of it in terms of the cosmic dance: it is the infinite God dancing with us finite creatures whom God loves dearly. He teaches us century after century the new things which we need to know, and teaches us century after century the impact of our sinfulness and selfishness on the world and cosmos.

These three attitudes and mindsets makes even more meaningful the prayer, "Glory to the Father, and to the Son and the Holy Spirit, as it was in the beginning, is now and will be forever. Amen."

These are some of the fruits of Centering Prayer. I am sure they sound familiar. They are found in any person's life who is open to the Spirit. As I said before so many times, the heart and soul of Centering Prayer is consent—consent to the presence and action of God in our lives. The prayer is simply an "I do," a consent, as pure and simple as anything can be in this life. And yet the willingness to say, "I do" to a commitment with the Lord is quite profound, in the spirit of Blessed Virgin Mary's *fiat*. Any fruits that come will come as a result of the power of consenting. Centering Prayer is a container holding our intention to consent, not only holding it but celebrating it. And in that celebration the Holy Spirit comes and may grant the gift of contemplative prayer. If that gift is granted, then in the words of Thomas Keating, there begins, "a process of interior transformation, a conversation initiated by God and leading, if we consent, to divine union."

10 ❊

Extending the Practice and Spreading the Word

I hope your reading of *Taste of Silence: Centering Prayer and the Contemplative Journey* has been a worthwhile experience. There is so much more I would like to share with you, but let me close with some hints on how to extend the practice into daily life. By now you are aware that Centering Prayer is not only a simple prayer practice but a key that opens you to the larger dimension of contemplative living. It is a prayer leading to your transformation into the image and likeness of God.

We need to do our part in cooperating with the Holy Spirit who has given us the grace to consent not only to God's presence in our lives but also God's action in our lives.

I think it is important that we create an environment that captures our desire to consent and leads us to a greater simplicity in our way of life—a desire for solitude and a comfort with silence. Allow me to make some comments about the following:

Most of us are part of a *church and faith community*. We have experienced the support of liturgy worship and ritual. We have our community prayer and private prayer. That never should change. The vast majority, including myself, need to know that we belong and are supported by others on our journey. Some people are able to sustain themselves on their own. That is great, but these people are the minority. If you think you can sustain yourself on your own, you may want to give this some consideration: you need support from a prayer partner or a group dedicated to Centering Prayer and its conceptual background. Otherwise, you will find your contemplative intentions sabotaged by your old habits as times goes on. It is not easy to make the time, because in reality we do not seem to have the time. The support of others is very important. So the first step in creating a contemplative environment is to join a group or get a prayer partner.

I was on a TV program called "The Christophers" a number of years ago. I was part of a panel with Fr. Thomas Keating and Mary Mrozowski. The moderator, Fr. Jack, asked Mary, "If this is a prayer where you sit in silence, why come together as a group to pray this way?" Mary answered, "Why not? Presence is the greatest gift and support on the journey. One another's presence in the prayer circle gives much support to us not only when we are together but also in those times when we pray on our own." I will never forget to look on Fr. Jack's face: he had never thought of the power of silent presence which comes through the united intention of each member. Picture this: a group of people, in a circle, in silence—sending up to heaven their silent hymn of glory as they are united in their consenting to God's presence and action in their lives. That is a powerful prayer, don't you think?

Lectio divina privately and in group. This is so vital. The Scriptures keep us grounded in our relationship with Jesus who is the Way, the Truth, the Light, and the Life. It is so easy to lose sight of the relational aspect of our journey. It is a personal relationship which is constantly calling us to greater intimacy with Christ. Some got so caught up in the silent sitting and receptivity that they began to forget not only their response to this relationship with Jesus but also to their responsibility to God, others, and themselves. The command is "Follow me." Follow means keeping our eyes (inner eyes) on the Other. Our eyes and ears must be open to this sacred following. When you have a chance, reread the chapter on *lectio divina.* Don't forget the four moments of the monastic *lectio*: to read, to ruminate, to respond, and to rest in the Word. Read it. When you read it, be with it. Taste it. Then pray from your heart and rest in its revelation to you. The bottom line is surrender. Don't rush through the reading. Every page has all you need; you have nowhere to hurry to. Don't just run to your favorite passages. Keep open so that you can become the word that you pray in the Scripture. The ultimate goal is to become what you read—that takes time. Make the time. Don't forget to pray *lectio divina* after Centering Prayer in group. It is a great support to your private *lectio*.

I would like to introduce a new idea at this point: it is the *active prayer.* The active prayers are those short prayer phrases that we carry with us each day. Gentle reminders, in a not-so-gentle world, that there is more going on here than meets the eye. Sometimes this active prayer may be a Scripture passage from our daily *lectio divina;* other times they could be a favorite prayer which we have carried with us from childhood like those aspirations and ejaculations such as, "My Lord and My God," "Jesus mercy," and "Mary the Mother of God, Pray for us." These short prayers said frequently throughout the day keep us conscious of the presence and action of God as we go about the activities of everyday life. They can be a pleasant and gentle reminder that "We are walking in the presence of the Lord in the land of the living" (Ps 116).

As a result of our consenting to God's presence and action in our lives there is a openness to the *purification and transformation process* that goes on each day. As I said earlier in discussing spirituality, as we accept the fact that we are animated by the Living Trinity within us, we will notice how we act and react habitually and spontaneously to the everyday events of our lives according to our vocation in life and our gifts. This ongoing awareness allows us to see what God wants us to see and hear. Whenever we notice that we are disproportionately responding to a situation, then we know that there is something here that we need to bring for forgiveness, for healing, or to bring to celebration. I like to see these moments as "actual graces"—special moments in which God nudges us, touches us, pushes us to see what needs to be done. How else is God's message going to get through to us except in the ordinary events of each day? I often laugh when I hear people say that God never sends them any messages or insights. If you feel that way it is because you are not looking in the right places. Look at each day, see how it goes, and don't miss the greatest adventure in life, daily living. You may be a little surprised by how you responded during the day. Then see if it has anything to do with those energy centers we talked about: power and control, affection and esteem, security and survival, or over-identification with your group. Reread the chapter on passive purification—it is a constant eye-opener. And again if you feel this does not apply to you, then just ask your loved ones if there are any things that you need to work on in your life—on second thought, don't do that unless you really want a rude awakening.

Centering Prayer is not only a communion with God but also a discipline. Discipline requires the establishing of new habits, new routines. Today with so many different exercise programs, most people are aware of the need for regular discipline. A certain period of time each day needs to be set apart in order to attain good health and well-being. This is also true on the spiritual journey. Time needs to be set apart and a regular daily program is important. It is recommended that one prays a twenty-minute period of Centering Prayer twice a day. Now I know that the initial reaction to this is, "When will I find the time?" I would suggest that for most it will require getting up earlier each day. "But I need my sleep." Yes, you do and you must have your sleep. I have a theory which has not been tested, but I believe it is worth considering. You have a choice. You can either approach the day gently by praying first and in a sense come into the new day with what I like to call a "gentle birth" or you can leap out of bed when the alarm rings, you hit the floor running, and begin the day with a feverish pace without time for prayer. I like to call this approach—"cesarean section." You are pulled out of the womb of the bed and tossed into the day fragmented right from the beginning. Is it any wonder that your day is shot to hell before it even begins? One interesting side benefit of Centering Prayer is that for many they need less sleep! It is a deeper rest than sleep. You must make the time; it has to be a priority. No one will make the time for you. There are always too many demands from others already. It is up to you: how important is this in your life?

People can't slow down. There is a standing joke circulating among my priest friends. We should not end mass with "Go in peace." We should end, "Ladies and Gentlemen, start your engines." And you would reply, "Thanks be to God, we can be off and running." Have you noticed what happens in the church parking lot after mass?

So I wish you well. Allow me to share one final comment. With the hectic pace of life of most of us, we need to ask for the grace to live in the present moment as we go about our daily activities. It is in living in the present moment that the contemplative dimension becomes a reality. If we go about our day stuck in some concerns about the past, whether it was an hour ago, a week ago, a month ago, or years ago, we give ourself two "gifts" —regret and guilt: regret about what has been done to us and guilt concerning what we did to another. If we go about our day stuck in what may happen in the future, we fill our day either with fear or anxiety: fear that we will get what we want but it will not be good for us, and anxiety that we will not get things the way we want.

The only moment we can really enjoy is the present moment. We can learn from the past, but we can't live there. We can plan for the future, but we can't live there. The only way we can really live is in the present. It is by being present to the present moment that we encounter our God and God encounters us. That is what the contemplative dimension of the gospel is all about in a "nutshell." "I will walk in the presence of the Lord in the land of the living." Moment, by moment, by moment, so help us, God.

◊ ◊ ◊

Spreading the Word

Beyond these suggestions I would like you to be aware of:

The Contemplative Outreach Prayer Program

An Introduction to Centering Prayer
Instruction of the Method of Centering Prayer, consisting of a one-day workshop (six hours) and six to twelve weekly sessions.

Lectio Divina and Its Movements into Contemplative Prayer
A workshop emphasizing an experience of the contemplative dimension of Scripture through the practice of *lectio divina*.

Centering Prayer Weekend Retreats and Intensive Days of Prayer
A retreat with increased periods of Centering Prayer and continuing education in the conceptual background.

Centering Prayer Intensive Retreats and Post Intensives
Seven-to-ten-day residential retreat with increased periods of Centering Prayer and viewing parts of *The Spiritual Journey* Video Tape Series, by Fr. Thomas Keating.

Formation for Contemplative Outreach Service
Preparing for commissioned presenters of the Introductory Workshop and for facilitators of Centering Prayer Groups.

For further information:
Contemplative Outreach Ltd. International Office
10 Park Place Suite 2-B
P.O. Box 737
Butler, NJ 07405
Phone (973) 838-3384 Fax: (973) 492-5795

Appendix ❈

The Method of Centering Prayer

Thomas Keating

Theological Background

THE GRACE OF Pentecost affirms that the risen Jesus is among us as the glorified Christ. Christ lives in each of us as the Enlightened One, present everywhere and at all times. He is the living Master who continuously sends the Holy Spirit to dwell within us to bear witness to His resurrection by empowering us to experience and manifest the fruits of the Spirit and the Beatitudes both in prayer and action.

Lectio Divina

Lectio divina is the most traditional way of cultivating friendship with Christ. It is a way of listening to the texts of Scripture as if we were in conversation with Christ and He were suggesting the topics of conversation. The daily encounter with Christ and reflection on His word leads beyond mere aquaintanceship to an attitude of friendship, trust, and love. Conversation simplifies and gives way to communing, or as Gregory the Great (sixth century), summarizing the Christian contemplative tradition, put it, "resting in God." This was the classical meaning of contemplative prayer for the first sixteen cenuries.

Contemplative Prayer

CONTEMPLATIVE PRAYER IS the normal development of the grace of baptism and the regular practice of *lectio divina*. We may think of prayer as thoughts or feelings expressed in words. But this is only one expression. Contemplative prayer is the opening of mind and heart — our whole being — to God, the Ultimate Mystery, beyond thoughts, words, and emotions. We open our awareness to God whom we know by faith is within us, closer than breathing, closer than thinking, closer than choosing — closer than consciousness itself. Contemplative prayer is a process of interior purification leading, if we consent, to divine union.

The Method of Centering Prayer

CENTERING PRAYER IS a method designed to facilitate the development of contemplative prayer by preparing our faculties to cooperate with this gift. It is an attempt to present the teaching of earlier time (e.g., *The Cloud of Unknowing*) in an updated form and to put a certain order and regularity into it. It is not meant to replace other kinds of prayer; it simply puts other kinds of prayer into a new and fuller perspective. During the time of prayer we consent to God's presence and action within. At other times our attention moves outward to discover God's presence everywhere.

The Guidelines

I. Choose a sacred word as the symbol of your intention to consent to God's presence and action within.

II. Sitting comfortably and with eyes closed, settle briefly and silently introduce the sacred word as the symbol of your consent to God's presence and action within.

III. When you become aware of thoughts, return ever-so-gently to the sacred word.

IV. At the end of the prayer period, remain in silence with eyes closed for a couple of minutes.

Explanation of the Guidelines

I. "Choose a sacred word as the symbol of your intention to consent to God's presence and action within." (cf. *Open Mind, Open Heart,* chap.5)

1. The sacred word expresses our intention to be in God's presence and to yield to the divine action.

2. The sacred word should be chosen during a brief period of prayer asking the Holy Spirit to inspire us with one that is especially suitable to us.
   a. Examples: *Lord, Jesus, Father, Mother, Mary;* or in other languages: Kyrie, Jesu, Jeshua, Abba, Mater, Maria.
   b. Other possibilities: *Love, Peace, Mercy, Silence, Stillness, Calm, Faith, Trust, Yes;* or in other languages: *Amor, Shalom, Amen.*

3. Having chosen a sacred word, we do not change it during prayer period, for that would be to start thinking again.

4. A simple inward gaze upon God may be more suitable for some persons than the sacred word. In this case, one consents to God's presence and action by turning inwardly to God as if gazing upon him. The same guidelines apply to the sacred gaze as to the sacred word.

II. "Sitting comfortably and with eyes closed, settle briefly and silently introduce the sacred word as the symbol of your consent to God's presence and action within."

1. By "sitting comfortably" is meant relatively comfortably; not so comfortably that we encourage sleep, but sitting comfortably enough to avoid thinking about the discomfort of our bodies during the time of prayer.

2. Whatever sitting position we choose, we keep the back straight.

3. If we fall asleep, we continue the prayer for a few minutes upon awakening if we can spare the time.

4. Praying in this way after a main meal encourages drowsiness. Better to wait an hour at least before Centering Prayer. Praying in this way just before retiring may disturb one's sleep pattern.

5. We close our eyes to let go of what is going on around and within us.

6. We introduce the sacred word inwardly and as gently as laying a feather on a piece of absorbent cotton.

III. "When you become aware of thoughts, return ever-so-gently to the sacred word."

1. "Thoughts" is an umbrella term for every perception including sense perceptions, feelings, images, memories, reflections, and commentaries.

2. Thoughts are a normal part of Centering Prayer.

3. By "returning ever-so-gently to the sacred word," a minimum of effort is indicated. This is the only activity we initiate during the time of Centering Prayer.

4. During the course of our prayer, the sacred word may become vague or even disappear.

IV. "At the end of the prayer period, remain in silence with eyes closed for a couple of minutes."

1. If this prayer is done in a group, the leader may slowly recite the Our Father during the additional two or three minutes, while the others listen.

2. The additional two or three minutes give the psyche time to readjust to the external senses and enable us to bring the atmosphere of silence into daily life.

Some Practical Points

1. The minimum time for this prayer is twenty minutes. Two periods are recommended each day, one first thing in the morning, and one in the afternoon or early evening.

2. The end of the prayer period can be indicated by a timer, provided it does not have an audible tick or loud sound when it goes off.

3. The principle effects of Centering Prayer are experienced in daily life, not in the period of Centering Prayer itself.

4. Physical symptoms:
   a. We may notice slight pains, itches, or twitches in various parts of our body or a generalized reslessness. These are usually due to the untying of emotional knots in the body.
   b. We may also notice heaviness or lightness in the extremities. This is usually due to a deep level of spiritual attentiveness.
   c. In either case, we pay no attention, or we allow the mind to rest briefly in the sensation, and then return to the sacred word.

5. *Lectio divina* provides the conceptual background for the development of Centering Prayer.

6. A support group praying and sharing together once a week helps maintain one's commitment to the prayer.

Extending the Effects of Centering Prayer into Daily Life

1. Practice two periods of Centering Prayer daily.

2. Read Scriptures regularly and study *Open Mind, Open Heart.*

3. Practice one or two of the specific methods for every day, suggested in *Open Mind, Open Heart,* chap. 12.

4. Join a Centering Prayer support group or follow-up program (if available in your area).
   a. It encourages the members of the group to persevere in private.
   b. It provides an opportunity for further input on a regular basis through tapes, readings, and discussion.

Points for Further Development

1. During the prayer period various kinds of thoughts may be distinguished. (cf. *Open Mind, Open Heart,* chap. 6–10):
   a. Ordinary wanderings of the imagination or memory.
   b. Thoughts that give rise to attractions or aversions.
   c. Insights and psychological breakthroughs.
   d. Self-reflections such as "How am I doing?" or, "This peace is just great!"
   e. Thoughts that arise from the unloading of the unconscious.

2. During this prayer we avoid analyzing our experience, harboring expectations, or aiming at some specific goal such as:
   a. Repeating the sacred word continuously.
   b. Having no thoughts.
   c. Making the mind blank.
   d. Feeling peaceful or consoled.
   e. Achieving a spiritual experience.

3. What Centering Prayer is not:
   a. It is not a technique.
   b. It is not a relaxation exercise.
   c. It is not a form of self-hypnosis.
   d. It is not a charismatic gift.
   e. It is not a para-psychological experience.
   f. It is not limited to the "felt" prescence of God.
   g. It is not discursive meditation or affective prayer.

4. What Centering Prayer is:
   a. It is at the same time a relationship with God and a discipline to foster that relationship.
   b. It is an exercise of faith, hope, and love.
   c. It is a movement beyond conversation with Christ to communion.
   d. It habituates us to the language of God which is silence.

Select Bibliography

Suggested Reading

Finley, James. *Merton's Palace of Nowhere* (Notre Dame, Ind.: Ave Maria Press 1978).

Hall, Thelma. *Too Deep For Words* (New York: Paulist Press, 1988).

Johnston, William, ed. *The Cloud of Unknowing* (New York: Image Book, 1973).

Keating, Thomas. *Intimacy with God* (New York: Crossroad, 1997).

———. *Invitation to Love* (New York: Continuum, 1997).

———. *The Mystery of Christ* (New York: Continuum, 1997).

———. *Open Mind, Open Heart* (New York: Continuum, 1998).

Nemeck, Francis, and Marie Theresa Coombs. *The Spiritual Journey: Critical Thresholds and Stages of Adult Spiritual Genesis* (Wilmington, Del.: Michael Glazier, 1988).

Pennington, Basil. *Centering Prayer* (New York: Doubleday, 1980).

Tugwell OP, Simon. *Ways of Imperfection: An exploration of Christian Spirituality* (Springfield, Ill: Templegate Publishers, 1985).

General Collections

Dupre, Louis, and James Wiseman, eds. *Light from Light: An Anthology of Christian Mysticism* (Mahwah, N.J.: Paulist Press, 1988).

Egan, Harvey, ed. *An Anthology of Christian Mysticism* (Collegeville, Minn, Pueblo Book,1991).

Magill, Frank N., and Ian P. McGreal, eds. *Christian Spirituality* (New York: Harper and Row, 1988).

Reading for Chapter 2

Bamberger, John Eudes, trans. *Praktikos and Chapters on Prayer* (Kalamazoo, Mich.: Cistercian Publications, 1970).

Beevers, John, trans. *Abandonment to Divine Providence* (New York: Doubleday Image Books, 1975).

Clarke, John, trans. *Story of a Soul: The Autobiography of St. Therese of Lisieux,* 2d ed. (Washington, D.C.: Institute of Carmelite Studies, 1976).

Evans, G.R., trans. *Bernard of Clairvaux: Selected Works* (Mahwah, N.J.: Paulist Press, 1987).

Ferfuson and Malherbe, trans. *Gregory of Nyssa: The Life of Moses* (Mahwah, N.J.: Paulist Press, 1978).

Kavanaugh, Kieran, and Otilio Rodriguez, trans. *The Collected Works of St. Teresa of Ávila* (Washington, D.C.: Institute of Carmelite Studies, 1991).

———, trans. *The Collected Works of St. John of the Cross* (Washington, D.C.: Institute of Carmelite Studies, 1979).

Luibheid, Colm, trans. *John Cassian: Conferences* (Mahwah, N.J.: Paulist Press, 1985).

Luibheid, Colm, and Norman Russell, trans. *John Climacus: The Ladder of Divine Ascent* (New York: Paulist Press 1982).

Pennington, Basil, *Thomas Merton, Brother Monk* (New York: Harper and Row, 1987).

Ryan, John, trans. *Introduction to the Devout Life* (New York: Doubleday, 1982).

Walsh, Edmund, and James Walsh SJ, trans. *Julian of Norwich: Showings* (Mahwah N.J.: Paulist Press 1978).

William of St. Thierry, *On Contemplating God, Prayer and Meditations,* trans. Theodore Berkeley, #3 (Kalamazoo, Mich: Cistercian Publications, 1971). Also *Golden Epistle* #13.

Wiseman, James, trans. *John Ruusbroec: The Spiritual Espousals and Other Works* (Mahwah, N.J.: Paulist Press, 1985).

THOMAS KEATING

OPEN MIND, OPEN HEART

Written by an acknowledged modern spiritual master, the book moves beyond "discursive meditation and particular acts to the intuitive level of contemplation." Keating gives an overview of the history of contemplative prayer in the Christian tradition, and step-by-step guidance in the method of centering prayer.

158 pages

THOMAS KEATING

THE MYSTERY OF CHRIST
The Liturgy as Christian Experience

A reflection on the contemplative dimension of Christian worship. Focusing on the liturgical year, Abbot Keating shares his theological and mystical perspective on the major feasts of the annual cycle.

160 pages

THOMAS KEATING

INVITATION TO LOVE
The Way of Christian Contemplation

In this final volume of his trilogy, Abbot Keating offers a road map, as it were, for a journey that begins when centering prayer is seriously undertaken.

160 pages

THOMAS KEATING

CRISIS OF FAITH, CRISIS OF LOVE
Revised and Expanded Edition

"Under the influence of Christian mystics such as St. John of the Cross, Keating weaves a narrative account of spiritual development that will be of . . . interest to spiritual directors and seekers."   —*Booklist*

140 pages

WILLIAM A. MENINGER

THE LOVING SEARCH FOR GOD
Contemplative Prayer and The Cloud of Unknowing

"Using the 14th-century spiritual classic *The Cloud of Unknowing* as both a jumping-off place and a sustained point of reference, Meninger, a Trappist monk and retreat master, does a powerful job of explaining contemplative prayer and making it approachable for any seeker. In a nurturing, practical and easy-to-understand manner, and with an obvious affection for his subject, Meninger deals with the yearning search for God through prayer and with the distractions that can impede it—unforgiveness and unforgivenness, will, distortions of imagination, memory, and intellect. The result, filled with humor and built by means of good, solid language that flows beautifully, is an excellent guide for anyone interested in deepening his or her Christian prayer life."

—*Publishers Weekly*

120 pages

WILLIAM A. MENINGER

THE PROCESS OF FORGIVENESS

In this book, Father Meninger explores the complex, but most necessary facet of spiritual life: forgiveness. He shows how we can learn to make this the most simple, yet most difficult part of our spiritual practice.

112 pages

WILLIAM A. MENINGER

THE TEMPLE OF THE LORD

And Other Stories

Composed in the form of three stories which form a triptych illustrating the spiritual life, the book examines three important facets of Christian understanding: "The Temple of the Lord," "Wisdom Built a House," and "The Messiah God."

96 pages

JOHN R. AURELIO

RETURNINGS

Life-after-Death Experiences: A Christian View

"Easy to read and full of practical insight."

—*Booklist*

"So, very good! What a strength and consolation this will be for many people!"
—Richard Rohr

120 pages

M. Basil Pennington

ON RETREAT WITH THOMAS MERTON

Fellow Cistercian monk and intimate friend of Merton, M. Basil Pennington wrote this book at Gethsemani Abbey where he lived in the hermitage where Merton spent his last five years. He offers an intimate glimpse of Merton's day-to-day living. With original photographs by Thomas Merton.

120 pages

M. Basil Pennington

THOMAS MERTON, BROTHER MONK

The Quest for True Freedom

"This is the Merton I knew—the seeker of God, the spiritual master. Each of the previous biographies has made its own unique contribution, but none has so explored the man's life. . . . a totally engaging and thoughtful work."

—James Finley

226 pages

Leonard J. Bowman

A RETREAT WITH ST. BONAVENTURE

Bowman explicates the life of the Franciscan Bonaventure (1217–1274) for modern-day applications of his teachings.

204 pages